Fragments of Memory

A Bilingual Poetry Collection
In English and Chinese

記憶的碎片
中英雙語詩選集

Phillip K. Lu
呂克華 著

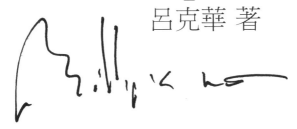

Cover: A 20x30" painting by the author
Designed by Charline Peng

記憶的碎片 Fragments of Memory

Amazon.com 經銷
2012年版權美國登記
未經授權不許翻印全文或部分
及翻印為其他語言或文字

Copyright ©2012 by Phillip K. Lu
All rights reserved
Including the right of reproduction and translation
In whole or in part in any form
without permission

Library of Congress Cataloging (applied for)
Manufactured in the United States

ISBN-13: 978-1456571962
ISBN-10: 1456571966

Preface and Introduction

I lived in a real world, through the brutal killing fields of WWII, the aftermath communist revolutions and the scientific blossom of the latter part of the 20th Century. While other teenagers enjoyed school, date, prom and free love, I struggled for survival, grown up in the adult world as a young boy in another world, subjected to prejudices, humiliations, discriminations and drifting amidst poverties, chaos and deaths. I ended growing up a righteous human being, a specialized scientist, studied, worked and taught in the most prestigious universities of the world. I wish to thank those who loved me and who had not abandoned me, even those who had deprived me of my youth, and those who had given me the strength to climb to a higher mountain.

I have no illusion in life, only reality. I worked extra diligently all my life just to keep me above water and to lead a straight life just to keep up with the steps of my fellow men. I fell down many times, but if I did, I just got up and maintained my heading towards my goal to achieve my objectives.

I do not consider my writing, including poetry, a creation; I consider it a way to create a new space and vista for me to explore and to capture all intangible reflections of my youth. While I have my limitations, my experiences, my struggles and my sufferings throughout my life have shaped me into what I am today. I think people who write poetry are not pessimistic or cynical; but many are hot-blooded individuals with sensitive and truthful honesty to themselves, and they held the principle that they believe what they do and think. As the American poet Czeslaw Milosz, Nobel Laureate in literature once wrote : "The history of the 20th Century prompted many poets to design images that convey their moral protest." Poetry reflects our living experiences, good or evil, love or hate. This world would be a wonderful world if we can recognize and overcome all those shortcomings.

This volume of bilingual poetry collection is similar to my first volume *Who Speaks for Me?*. I continue to probe my inner identity, perhaps, at the same time to expose my personal character. I am indebted to Dr. Hong-yee Chiu, who has contributed many valuable comments and techniques of editing and formatting a book.

December, 2012 Bethel, CT

序言與介紹

　　我生活在一個真實的世界，經過二次世界大戰的殘酷殺害，共產主義革命與二十世紀後期的科學興旺時期。當其他少年正在享受學業，交往男女朋友，中大學的跳舞晚會，和自由戀愛。我卻在另一個世紀為生存而掙扎與奮鬥，一位年輕男孩在成人的世界裡成長，受到偏見，屈辱和歧視，走在貧窮，動亂與和死亡的道路之間。我成長為一位非常公正的人，受過高等教育專門從事的科學家，在世界上有名望的大學裡學習，工作和教學。我感謝那些愛我及沒有遺棄我的人，包括那些剝奪了我青少年經歷而不能去渡過的人，我感謝那些助長我攀登更高一座山力量的人。

　　在生命中我沒有幻覺僅有現實。為了要跟得上別人的步驟與保持志高氣揚，行為正直，我勤奮的努力一生。在我跌倒之後，我站起來再繼續奮鬥，仍然維護我的途徑及目標去完成我的使命。

　　我不認為我的寫作，包括寫詩，是創作;它僅是為我創造一個自由的空間去探索和奪回我的青年時期所有的感想。當我在實際生活的領域有所限制，我的經驗，我的奮鬥和我在生活裡的折磨塑造成我的今天。我認為寫詩的人都不一定全是悲觀或者是憤世嫉俗，只是一些充滿熱血敏銳的人物，對他們自己誠實，對原則與對他們的相信真實。如獲得諾貝爾獎的美國著名詩人秘羅茲曾經說：「二十世紀的歷史提示許多詩人去表達和描述他們對道德的抗議。」詩反應我們生活中的經驗，善或惡，愛或恨。如果我們可以承認和克服所有那些缺點，這個世界也許能是一個美妙好的世界。

　　這卷雙語詩選集與我第一冊《誰為我說話？》的詩集相同。我繼續的探索我內在的本體，或許，同時也暴露了我個人的品格。我很感激丘宏義博士，他在整個寫作，編排與校訂過程中指導甚多。

2012 年十二月康州柏索鎮

About the Author

An astronomer turns to writer. Born in China in a peasant family, He left home at the age of 12 to find work, then joined an Artillery Youth Training Regiment. During the civil war, he drifted from place to place in southeast China with the regiment and eventually settled in Taiwan.

He came to America nearly 50 years ago to pursue graduate studies and received his MA degree from Wesleyan University, Middletown, CT., and Ph.D. in astronomy from Columbia University in New York City. He did several years of pre- or post-graduate researches at Yale and Wesleyan Universities, then taught and conducted research in astronomy at Western Connecticut State University for 30 years. During his tenure as Chairman and Distinguished Professor of Astronomy, he has received numerous grants and awards from the National Science Foundation and other agencies. He has published nearly 100 research papers in Astronomical and Astrophysical Journals, compiled a two volume set of Yale Zone Star Catalogs (Yale University Press), edited conference proceedings, "The Gravitational Force Perpendicular to the Galactic Plane" with D. Philip (L. Davis Press), "The New Age of Exploration: Next 500 Years" (WCSU University Press), He also translated the late Carl Sagan's "Cosmos" from English to Chinese with Hong-Yee Chiu (Yuanliou Books), received Dr. Da-Yu Wu's Science Writer Prize, a prize in honor the late President of the Academy of Science, 2006 and "How to Make Telescopes" also with H.Y. Chiu (Chung Cheng Books).

After his retirement from teaching, he rejoined the Astronomy Department, Yale University to continue his research for a few more years. Then began his passion of listening to classical music, reading and writing poetry and joining a Creative Writing group to enrich his writing skill. His poems and other essays have been published in various publications, such as Noble House, London, UK and the International Library of Poetry.

作者簡介

　　天文學家轉為作家。出生在中國一個農民家庭，十二歲為找工作而離家，然後參加炮兵青年訓練營。在內戰期間他流浪在中國東南，然後隨軍隊撤移到臺灣定居。

　　四十多年前他來美國天文研究所進修，在美國康涅狄格州衛斯理楊大學獲得天文物理學碩士學位之後，在紐約市哥倫比亞大學獲得科學教育碩士及天文學博士學位。在耶魯大學和衛斯理楊大學做了幾年研究，然後在康州西方州立大學開始他在天文教學及研究 30 年。曾任物理及天文系教授及系主任，獲得美國科會研究獎及其他研究基金。1991 年命名為天文傑出教授。他在天文學和天體物理學報期刊曾發表研究論文約 100 篇。耶魯大學《恆星固有運動星表》二冊(耶魯大學出版)，編輯天文學專題討論會議論文有《銀河重引力垂直銀河平面》(與大衛菲利普合著，大衛斯出版社)及《未來 500 年的新探險》(西康州立大學出版)。從英語翻譯到漢語的書籍包括卡爾薩根的《宇宙 宇宙》(與丘宏義合譯，遠流出版)，2006 年與丘宏義榮獲故科學院院長吳大猷博士基金會的科學作家獎)及和丘宏義合著《如何做望遠鏡》(中正書店出版)。

　　退休之後，他再回到耶魯大學天文系，繼續他的研究數年，然後才開始聽他熱愛的古典音樂，閱讀中英詩歌名著和其他散文及文學傳記與寫作，多年前，他參加柏索鎮創意寫作小組去增進他寫作的知識及技術，曾多次發表於中美刊物，其中包括英國倫敦皇家出版社和國際詩歌圖書。

目錄/Content

I. Imperfect Stance/不完美的姿態   2

Imperfect Stance/不完美的姿態   4-6
Fading yet Unyielding/衰老而不屈服   8
Moonlight and I/月光與我   10
Charcoal and Flower/花與木炭   12
From Where I Stand/從我站的地方   14
Ripple/漣漪   16
Benign Occurrences/無作輕重的發生   18
My Song/我的歌   20
Identity/身份   22
Absence and Presence/缺席與列席   24
Continuity/連續性   26
Spring Welcome/春天的歡迎   28
Our Castle/我們的城堡   30
Out Patience's Surgery/門診部手術   32
Fragments of Illusion/幻覺的片段   34
Aging /年齡的效應   36
Independence Day Extreme/國慶日的極端   38
Old Cats/老貓   40
Uneasy in the Big Easy/大易的不易   42
Clay Monk Crossing River/泥和尚過河   44
Rights of Citizenship/公民權   46-8
A late Bloomer/大器晚成者   50
Gabbles in Late Spring/晚春片語   52
Benign Syndrome/無作為症狀   54
Passive Reaction/被動的反應   56
Sharing Space/分享空間   58
Natural State/自然狀態   60
Our World and Our Life/我們的世界與生活   62
Never Ending Struggle/無止境的掙扎   64
Elusive Fate/無從捉摸的命運   66
Ultimate Redemption/最終的贖罪   68
Premonition/預誡   70
Spring Fever/春季的熱潮   72
Metaphor/隱喻   74

II. Life Perspectives/生命的透視　　　　　76

Rats Year Mentality/鼠年的意識　　　　　78
Objective and Subjective Reality/客觀與主觀的現實　80
From my Vantage Point/從我處於有利的論點　82
Gibberish on the Vernal Equinox/春分隨筆　84
April Fools' Essay/愚人節的漫筆　　　　　86
Scrutinized Experiences/徹查的經驗　　　88
Death and Transfiguration/死亡和變形　　90
Restless/心神不定　　　　　　　　　　　92
Amorphous Entity/無形的個體　　　　　　94
Truth and Validity/真理與正確　　　　　　96
Scale of Morality/道德的尺度　　　　　　98
Illusion Versus Reality/幻覺與現實　　　　100
Individuality/獨立性　　　　　　　　　　102
Wandering in the Mist/在薄霧中漫遊　　　104
Words in Forest/在森林裡的字詞　　　　　106
Taxonomy of Seeds/種子的分類　　　　　108
Dents in Illusion/在幻覺裡的凹痕　　　　　110
Tidbits of Andes/安地斯的拾零　　　　　　112-4
A Sense of Flatness/一種蕭條的感受　　　116-8
Hope in Humanity/人類還有希望　　　　　120-2
If I do not Wake up/如果我醒不過來　　　124
Life Perspectives/生命的透視　　　　　　126
Pretending Tendency/妄想的趨勢　　　　　128
Essence/本質　　　　　　　　　　　　　130
Prospective Changing/預期的改變　　　　132
Chess Game Analogy/一盤棋賽的比喻　　　134
Symbolic View/象徵性的觀點　　　　　　136
Disparity in Metamorphosis/變體的差距　　138
Pigments of Elation/振奮的顏料　　　　　140
A Wisp of Breeze/一絲微風　　　　　　　142
The Alchemy of Sentiment/情操的魔力　　　144
A Gasping Bull/吳牛喘月　　　　　　　　146
Poetics of Nothingness/微不足道的詩　　　148
Beyond Geriatrics/老年醫學之外　　　　　150
Pseudo Bleeding Heart/半真假的傷心　　　152
A Common Man/一個普通人　　　　　　154
Nostalgia/鄉愁　　　　　　　　　　　　156
A Year-end Reflection/年尾的回顧　　　　158-0

III. New Beginning/新的開始	162
A New Year as I see it/我所看見的新年	164
Life Without Form/沒有形式的生命	166
Truth has its Own Style/真理有它自己的形式	168
Early Spring Thaw/早春的溶解	170
The Spirit of Moths/飛蛾的精神	172
The Dust of Changing Time/時間變化的塵埃	174
With Borrowed Wings/借用了肢翼	176
Redemption for Free Verses/自由詩的贖罪	178
Cradles/搖籃	180
Stanza of Mixed Cradle/混合詩節的搖籃	182
Clumsiness is Talent/笨拙也是才幹	184
No Consequences/無足輕重	186
Skewed Observation/歪曲的觀察	188
Best Medicine/良藥	190
Passing Gale/一陣風	192
Zenist's Traits/禪教信徒的特色	194
A Song of Pre-destiny/預定命運的歌曲	196
Naked Metaphor/赤裸的隱喻	198
The Corridor of Time/時間流逝的走廊	200
Thieves of Nature/自然的竊賊	202
Counterpart/相對性	204
Overtures of my Indulgence/縱情前奏曲	206-8
Autumn Leaves/秋葉	210
Yours or Mine/你的還是我的	212
Gateway of Spirit/心靈的通道	214
Not to be Outdone/不認輸	216
Uncertain Steps/不稳的步伐	218
Not a Coincidence/不是巧合	220
Anachronistic Vibration/不適時代的激動	222
An Allegory/寓言	224
Impractical Heart/不切實際的身心	226
Transient Farewell/匆匆而過的告別	228
A Civilized Zoo/文明的動物園	230
Imperceptibly Certain/感覺不到的可靠性	232
An Observation/觀察	234
An Un-annealed Critic/一個未韌化的評論	236
A Writer's Lamentation/作者的悲歌	238

A Pre-holiday Sentiment/一個假日前的情操   240
Winter Solstice's Interjection/冬至的感嘆   242
Worthiness of Man/人之可敬   244
Faceless Domain/面目不明的領域   246
Once in a Blue Moon/罕見的時機   248

Crab Nebula- a Supernova

A. three dimension woodcut mounted on acylice painting, 24"x30 ", by the author

To my family

一. 不完美的姿態

我們不完全是絕對被動，
我們的身體，意識，思維，
和精神是不斷活動，
說是現在，已經是太遲，
說我們青年我們已經有點老化，
說我們在一起，
除了在親密的關頭時刻，
我們永遠不可能佔用同一空間。
...
在自然與詩人之間，
他們的音樂是秘密。

I. **Imperfect Stance**

We are not absolutely passive,
Our body, awareness, consciousness
and spirit are constantly active.
To say now, it is already too late,
To say we are young, we have aged,
To say we are here together,
Except in the moment of intimacy,
We could never occupy the same space.
…
Between a poet and nature,
The music is a secret.

191　不完美的姿態

混亂的雨聲，
結合我規律搏動
的心臟，
當我的頭碰到柔軟的枕頭，
珍貴的一天
也就目光短淺的消散。
我向我平淡無事
的收場致敬，
在我明晨甦醒之前，
含糊的期間擺佈我的思維。

缺席與列席相互排除，
空間和時間是共存與相對，
在沙漠中開始行程有起點，
在沙裡那兒畫線，
它只是旅行者的引喻，
對沙地沒有一點區分。

攀登高峰
或潛入海洋，
探測未知
是令人振奮，多高和多深
我們能抵達是有限，只有
「天頂」與「深淵」是無界限，
它們有抽象引用的條件，
很少有經驗的或實用關係，
最後的基準點
乃是我們自己。

我們生活
在一個不完美的社會，
那有真正措施的同位，
富裕的少數通常具有優勢，
赤貧永遠是沒有什麼特權，
多麼妄想
我們相信它們的平等，
此類的對照
有如小丘比高山。

191 **Imperfect Stance**

The chaotic sound of rain,
Orchestrating the regular throbs
of my heartbeat,
When my head hits the soft pillow,
A specious day is
improvidently ended.
I salute my uneventful
conclusion of the day.
Before I wake tomorrow morning,
An ambiguous period manipulates me.

Absence and presence are mutually exclusive,
Space and time are relative and coexist,
A journey begins in desert has an origin,
Where, the line is drawn in the sand,
It is only an allusion to the travelers,
It does not make a difference to the sand.

Climbing to a summit
or diving into an ocean,
The exploration into the unknown
is exhilarating, how high or deep
we can reach is limited, only
zenith or *abyss* is limitless.
They are abstract references in context,
With little empirical or pragmatic relevance,
The ultimate point of reference
is still in us.

We do not
 live in a perfect society,
There is no true measure in parity.
The affluent few are always with advantages,
The destitute are forever without privileges,
What an illusion
we believe there is equality,
The analogy is comparing
mountains with hills.

5

在這裡，我像瘋子一樣的亂寫，
忽略雨果和惠特曼，
的寶貴美德，
艾蜜莉狄金生的保守主義，
聶魯達熱愛的海洋和智利，
秘魯茲的人道主意觀，
和中國典型四行詩句。

文字，像些小魚，
在我的頭裡游來游去，
我用我的手指把它們撈出。
血腥的音節，汗水與眼淚一齊，
點點滴滴，
從一種媒介到另一種介體，
從柔軟的皮肉，落進水晶記憶體，
可悲的仍是啞口無言。

我們不完全是絕對被動，
我們的身體，意識，思維，
和精神是不斷活動，
說是現在，已經是太遲，
說我們青年我們已經有點老化，
說我們在一起，
除了在親密的關頭時刻，
我們永遠不可能佔用同一空間。

詩人不使用帆布和畫筆，
他們也能製造生動的像影。
自然純淨及華麗的圍攏著我們，
與她共存是一種安慰和治療。
我們不必要題寫她的意向，
只要閉上您的眼睛呼吸新鮮空氣，
他們像詩詞是一樣的強而有力，
在自然與詩人之間，
他們的音樂是秘密。

2003 年 11 月

Here, I write like a mad man,
Ignoring the golden virtues,
Of Victor Hugo and Walt Whitman,
Emily Dickenson's conservatism,
Neruda's love of Chile and ocean,
Czeslaw Milosz's humanistic view,
And the typical Chinese quatrain poems.

Words, like little fishes,
Swimming in my head,
I fish them out through my fingers.
Bloody syllables, together with sweat and tears,
Dripping and dropping,
From one medium to another,
From soft tissues into the chips of memory,
Sadly voiceless.

We are not absolutely passive,
Our body, awareness, consciousness
and spirit are constantly active.
To say now, it is already too late,
To say we are young, we have aged,
To say we are here together,
Except in the moment of intimacy,
We could never occupy the same space.

Poets do not use paintbrushes and canvas,
Images they create are just as vivid.
Natures surround us innocently and gay,
Coexist with them, soothing and therapeutic.
We do not have to inscribe their intent,
Just close your eyes breathe in fresh air,
They are as powerful as poetic verses.
Between a poet and nature,
The music is a secret.

Nov. 2003, rev. 2011

164　衰老而不屈服

我們年輕的時候都想離家，
老年的時候又渴望回鄉，
避免孤獨你要學會寧靜，
只相信別人所說的一半，
明智的知道哪一半可信。

我越來越少看見熟悉的面孔，
目睹越來越多奇怪的幻影，
在我的世界這沒有什麼奇異，
在二維*事件視界*的確定之 間，
花開之後又枯萎變得含糊。

我仍然在這裡好像倔強的雪松，
在如此荒涼的環境中堅定支撐，
大多數我的親友都已消失。
而我卻增長得挑戰及大膽，
有敏銳的感覺，拒絕退讓。

他們說您須要朋友才能向前，
您需要仇敵才能成功。
友誼好像是駝絨被，
敵意像是冷的僵硬枕頭，
只有您自己的身體才能保持您溫暖。

在這個宇宙我學會一點點，
曾在公海上航行。
在海洋和天際之間，
撒種子和傳播啟發，
但只有少數開花結果。

我仍然是不屈不撓和心情開朗，
善於和土壤和植物連接，
但不能與社會保持交往，
我不再行走以前經過的路道，
只相信好馬不吃回頭草。

164   **Fading yet Unyielding**

We elope from home young,
Longing to return when we are old,
To avoid loneliness is learning to be lonely,
Believe only half of what people say,
Be wise to know which half is believable.

I see fewer and fewer familiar faces,
And more and more strange apparitions,
It is not that unusual in my world,
Between two event-horizons of certainty,
Flowers blossom then wither into obscurity.

I am still here like intractable cedar,
Standing firm in such bleak surroundings,
Most of my relations have faded away.
It is I who have grown bold and defiant,
Having a keen sense, refusing to yield.

They say you need friends to get ahead,
And you require foes to be successful.
Friendship is like a comforter,
Enmity is as cold as a stiff pillow,
Only your own body will keep you warm.

I learned a few things in this cosmos,
Having navigated in the open sea,
In between oceans and realms of space,
Spreading inspirations and sowing seeds,
Only a few bear fruit and blossom.

I am still resilient and gay,
Good in dealing with soil and plants,
But poor keeping social acquaintances,
I hardly walk the path after I have passed,
Believing a horse does not eat grass behind its heel.

022　月光與我

我返鄉探望我的家，
但是那裡沒有人煙。
月光泛灘我四周的萬物，
而我跌倒在自己的影子裡，
但沒有其他的陰影，
在我身影的附近。

那株孤獨老樹是我唯一的伴侶，
但是我既不理解它的音樂和它的歌唱，
也不領悟它的語言。
除了聽見有人在歎息，
那是風聲還是我的哭泣？

寒冷夜晚的空氣擁抱著我，
但是我沒有任何人可以擁抱。
月光想要領導我離去，
但是，我無處可去，
只有陷入在我自己的憂鬱。

月光了解我的寂寞，
但她不能減輕我的疼痛和悲傷，
月光和我呼叫憐憫，
但是沒有人聽見我們 的抱怨，
除了我們傾聽風的叫喊。

1988 年 11 月 18 日

　　一九八八年十一月，在一個月光明亮的夜晚，我第二次返回安徽省來安縣老家訪問。我們原來的房舍已經不在那裡，雙親都已去逝。我是單獨一個人，寂寞和沮喪。除了月光照著萬物和我之外，在院子的當中站立著一棵老柳樹及不斷的風聲。

022   **Moonlight and I**

> I return visiting my home,
> But there is no home.
> Moonlight floods everything around me,
> And I fall on to my own shadow,
> But there are not other shadows
> near me.
>
> The lonely old tree is my only companion,
> But I neither understand her language,
> Nor comprehend her music and sing,
> Except I hear someone's sigh,
> Is that weeping by me or the wind?
>
> The chilly night air embraces me,
> But I have no one to embraces with.
> Moonlight wishes to lead my way,
> But, I have no place to go,
> Only immerse in my own melancholy.
>
> Moonlight understands my lonesome,
> But she could not ease my sadness and pain.
> Moonlight and I cry for compassion,
> But there is no one to hear our complaints,
> Except we listen the howling of wind.
>
> Nov. 18, 1988

I wrote this verse during my second visit of my old home in November 1988, Anhui, China. Our original house was no longer there and both of my parents passed away. I was alone, lonesome and depressed. Other than the bright moonlight floods everywhere around me, there was an old willow tree standing in mid of wind.

176　花與木炭

每人都熱切的慶祝成功，
很少人寬恕你的失敗，
有些人忍受緊迫只是為了合群，
其他的更為榮耀錦上添花。
那是為了歡樂中的，
葡萄酒及乳酪？
或只是顯耀，
你的首飾及服裝。

勝利常與慶祝同當，
失敗跟隨的總是絕望，
光榮是讓人人來分享，
失敗只有你個人；
來承當！

親戚們在生活中幾乎不常見，
只是在悲哀的場合碰個面。
如果孩子們不給你做生日，
他們一定會有一個埋葬後的接見。

誰關心那最後告別的扮演？
和那不關緊要的慰勉。
一些人生動的詳述著死者的慈善，
其他的人給予無情的促進。

為什麼你不在寒冬下雪的夜晚，
贈送木炭為禮物，
而在棺材上拋下眼淚與薔薇。

2003 年 7 月 15 日

　　「花與木炭」的標題來自中國一句有名的成語(誰會雪中送炭，只有錦上添花)。在現代社會裡的人也有同樣的傾向。而不給那些失落身心的人一點憐憫。(英文在 2003 年《最佳詩與詩人》發表，國際詩集圖書，第一頁)

176   Charcoal and Flower

Everyone is eager celebrating success,
But few condone your failure,
Some endure stress just to be social,
Others add flowers to the brocade for the glory.
Is it because wine and cheese
in the festivity?
Or just to show off
your costumes and jewelries.

Victory usually comes with celebration,
Defeat is often followed by despair,
Glory is for everyone to share,
Failure is only for you to bear;
Alone!

Relatives hardly get together in life,
Only meet when there is a sad occasion.
If children don't give you a birthday party,
There is always a post burial reception.

Who cares for the final act of farewell?
Or the small talks of condolences.
Some discuss vividly the humanity of the dead,
Others offer cold-hearted encouragements.

Why don't you send the gift of charcoal?
In the snowy nights of bitter winter,
Rather shed tears and lay roses on the coffin.

July 15, 2003

The title of 'Charcoal and Flower' comes from a famous Chinese classical idiom (Who will send charcoal in the snowy weather, only to add flowers to the brocade.) People in this modern society are likely to do the same and not to shed any pity to those unfortunate souls. English first appeared in *The Best Poems and Poets in 2003*, International Library of Poetry.

201　從我站的地方

藍天在我的頭上，
青草在我的腳下，
我在可見領域的中心，
與一切事物包圍著我。

我的頭飄蕩在浮雲之間，
我的腳樹立在地面，
有如一顆發芽的種子。

我夾在上天優雅的下方，
和地面上的醜惡及骯髒，
搜尋希望結尾是一場空。

我不在任何人管轄下，
環境使我不停的流浪，
以往的視覺消失無影無蹤，
新的挑戰出現我必須抵抗。

仔細眺望我的四方，
看見事大事小，
有的出眾有的微不足道。

你不要只看他們的服裝及顏色；
和那偽造的外表，
剝去表面上的掩飾，
我們都是同樣的晦暗及單調。

2004 年 1 月 1 日

　　我從未有過新年的宣言，我認為那只是愚人的決定。可是，我常常會要提醒我自己，在這個冷酷無情，及人們表面虛假的社會。

201   From Where I Stand

Blue sky is over my head,
Green grasses under my feet,
I am at the center of my visible realm,
With all entities surrounds me.

My head is in the cloud,
My feet plant on earth,
Like shoot sprouts from a seed.

I wedged in between the grace above,
And the ugly and filthy below,
Searching for aspiration ended with null.

I am in no one's keeper,
And circumstances move me vagrant,
Past vision disappears into void,
New challenge appears for me to defend.

Carefully survey my surroundings,
To see some small and some grand,
Others are eminent or insignificant.

You do not look them as what they are,
With synthetic costumes and colors,
Strip off the surface camouflage,
We are all equally dull and monotonous.

Jan 1, 2004

    I have never made any New Year's resolution and thought such resolution is only the fools' solution. However, I often warn myself the harshness of world and the synthetic outer surface of people.

209　漣漪

多麼光彩的一片金色田園，
對應著小山後的藍天，
飛雲製造了陰影，
把原野染成彩色的陰影。

我就像飛雲一樣的平靜，
沈默地陶醉在草原裡，
我以為我擁有全部的景色，
如同我所聞、感受和所見。

一位少女出現在小山上，
柔和地聲音來自她的歌唱，
她的衣裙頭髮溫和地在風中飄蕩，
微風吹來她身上的芬芳。

她如同草園中的一朵野花，
或是這壯麗景觀的一部分，
啊!在畫像裡面是誰的女兒?
在我無波腦海裡增加一點漣漪。

2004 年 4 月 1 日

209   **Ripple**

What a splendid golden field,
Against the blue sky over the hills,
Shadows created by the flying clouds,
Paint the field into colorful shades.

I am peaceful as the passing clouds,
Silently indulge in the pastures.
I thought I own the entire scenery,
As what I smell, feel and behold.

A young maiden appears on the hill,
Soft singing comes from her voice,
Her skirt and hair flirt gently in wind,
Breeze brings in her sweet fragrance.

She is as if one of the wild flowers,
Or a part of the magnificent landscape,
O! Whose daughter is there in portrait?
To add a few ripples in my peaceful stance.

April 1, 2004 April fool's Day

197　無作輕重的發生

對您，我是一個灰白頭髮的老人，
曾經是一個反抗父母和命運的男生，
很少人知道我是被推崇的科學教授，
但在街上卻是一個愚笨的中國人，
認識我就完全改變你的觀感，
我的氣概與正直是我的表徵。

我穿的和擁有只是表面，
一個沒有品質外在的出現，
我的成功與失敗都有公開的紀錄，
我既不會乞求稱讚也不需要饒恕，
要知道我的氣質和本性，
您必須要瞭解我的品格。

對我，它是一種榮譽和責任，
悲傷流淚去安葬您的父母，
海洋和河流吞沒了我的本能，
政治界限使我無能奮勇，
我無特殊榮幸補償我最後的敬意，
此種行為給我留下終生的遺憾。

在這個我行我素的世界，
我們忙著搜尋舒適和財富，
誰有心情去煩惱父母的需求？
或是為他們的困境真正的哀傷，
偶爾在墓碑附近獻花是一種奢侈，
我們甚至於沒有灰甕埋葬的可能。

由於愛戀和土地的缺乏，
氣化您的骨肉即將會現實，
一片簡單的木板象徵您的生存，
或是一本被忽略姓名的登記簿。
沒有保留的遺體為了你的復活，
您的靈魂就像秋霧一樣的漂浮。

2008 年 5 月 11 日

197   **Benign Occurrences**

To you, I am an old man with grey hair,
Once a defiant boy to his parent and his fate,
Few knew I was an esteemed professor of science,
But a dumb Chinese on the street,
Knowing me make all the difference,
My spirit and integrity is my trade.

What I wear and possess is superficial,
An outer appearance without qualities,
My success and failure are in public records,
I beg neither for forgiveness nor for praise.
To know my temperament and nature,
You will have to decipher my character.

To me, it is an honor and responsibility,
To bury your parent with sorrow and tears,
Oceans and rivers devoured my capabilities,
Political boundaries made it impossibility,
I have no privilege to pay my last respect,
The bad deed has left me life-long regret.

In this world of self-imposed approaches,
We are busy searching for comfort and riches,
Who have the heart to worry about parental needs?
Be thoughtfully and genuinely sad for their demise,
Flowers near tombstone occasionally are luxury,
We may not even have ashes and urn to bury.

With the scarcity of affection and burial land,
Vaporizing your flesh is a soon-to-be reality,
A simple plaque symbolizes your existence,
Or an entry lists the volumes of neglected registry.
There is no physical remain for your resurrection,
And your soul is drifting like autumn mist.

May 11, 2008

222 我的歌

我看見光譜所有的醜惡及優美,
用我的舌頭去嚐試酸甜苦辣,
我聞過一陣惡臭及芳香,
聽得見寂靜及大聲響。

我沒有選擇氣味的來源,
但卻喜歡傾聽悅耳的歌唱。

我是我自己決策的主子,
也是我自己慾望的牧羊,
無人全能控制他們的命運,
時運及天命玩弄他們的花樣。

我從不希望去統治這個世界,
但也不願別人奴役我的思想。

我每次講的都是實情,
決不希望去迷惑欺詐他人,
我的頭腦直接去指導我的行為,
以嚴厲的機智去執行我所設想。

我以禮貌去善待所有的人,
但也從不接收無理的責難。

我的耳朵聽的不僅是音樂,
也同樣聽見在我耳後的謊,
我感到冷熱是看我如何的被對待,
但不能防禦無情的冷淡。

欣賞甜美是人的天性,
厭惡惡劣的品格是來自希望。

2004 年 7 月 11 日

222   **My Song**

I see the spectrum of ugly and beauty,
Taste sweet and bitter with my tongue,
I smell the puffs of stench and fragrance,
And hear both the silence and sound.

I have no choice to the incoming odor,
But do prefer to hear the joyful song.

I am my own master in decision,
Shepherd of my own longing and desire,
No one can totally control their own fate,
Fortune and destiny manipulate their own.

I never wish to dominate this world,
Nor wish anyone enslaving my mind.

I speak with truth and validity,
Never wish to mislead and deceive anyone,
My brain directly direct my action,
And act with stern will what I have planned.

I will bestow everyone with courtesy,
But do not accept any unreasonable blame.

My ears listens not only music,
But also derogatory remarks from behind,
I feel hot and cold by how I was treated,
But cannot prevent the chills of unkind.

Enjoy pleasant and beauty are by nature,
And disgust foul behavior is by desire.

July 11, 2004

271　身份

在黑暗纖細的空間，
萬哩以外及無數個光年，
那兒缺少幅射及重力，
我既無影像又無身份，
沒有路線、邊界及目的，
也許那才是自由真正的意義。

我僅有生存的證據，
只是我誠摯生命的舉止，
和我的英勇及藐視。

在無可能性中的可能，
在毀滅中的創立，
不斷的向新的境界進行。

我所做的消失無痕跡，
我所說消散去空虛。

一切事物變得都不存在，
無物與萬物結合在一起，
世界從不會如你的察覺，
只有你自己的神志才是實體。

2005年3月5日

　　生活在這個虛假的世界，我們常常喪失我們自己的本體。我們去蒙蔽別人，甚至於我們自己只是為了要能和我們的環境與社會打成一片. 我們所說和所為都變得不恰當，我們所達到的成就，一樣能由欺詐而喪失.

271 **Identity**

In the midst of dark, tenuous space,
Billions of miles and light-years away,
Lack of radiation and gravity,
I have neither image nor identity,
Aimless, without boundary and path,
Perhaps that is the true meaning of free.

The only proof of my existence,
Is by my earnest behavior of being,
And by my courage and my defiance.

Impossibility is possibility,
Destruction is creation,
Constantly evolve into new realms.

What I have done vanished without a trace,
What I said dissipated into void,

Everything is becoming nothing,
Nothing is integrated with everything.
The world never ends as you may perceive,
Only your own conscious is the reality.

March 5, 2005

We often lose our own identity to live in this fictitious and wishy-washy world. In order just to be fitted into our environment and society, we deceive others and even ourselves. What we say and do become irrelevant. What we have achieved may be also lose by deception.

285　缺席與列席

我閉上眼睛，
來保護我的直覺，
而不去浪費我的視力，
我阻塞我的耳朵，
來保存聽覺，
而不去聽那些醜惡的謊言，
我掉轉頭去避免瞞騙欺詐，
可憐的行為及偽裝，
但不改變途徑，
由於挑戰與荊棘擱置在前。

惡棍曾經打擊過我，
我卻拒絕向平凡低頭，
我仍然在這裡防禦我的正直，
真正的力量，
將在最後得勝，
我仍然在此防範我的善行，
情勢試圖剝削我的敬重，
沒有職業和責任的負擔，
光榮與成功只是暫時的興奮。

誠實的聖殿無處可尋，
欺詐侵略了我們道德的真誠，
經過這些，
模糊的領域，
或許我已變得明智與沾沾自喜，
平靜的生活有許多種形式，
我們不必要總是完美，
和在所有戰爭中得勝，
缺席與列席相互存在。

2005 年 4 月 1 日

修訂詩篇-取自《誰為我說話》詩集

285   **Absence and Presence**

I shut my eyes
to save my perception,
In order not to waste my eyesight,
I block my ears
to conserve my hearing,
instead listening those filthy lies,
I turn my head to avoid deception,
pitiful acts and disguise,
But do not change my path,
Due to challenge and thorns lay ahead.

I have been beaten by thugs,
Yet refuse to bow to the mediocrity,
The real strength will prevail
in the end.
I am still here to defend my virtue,
Circumstances try to strip my esteem.
I have tasted sense of freedom,
Without burden of duty and profession,
Glory and success are transient.

I fail finding sanctuary of honesty,
Deception has invaded our moral integrity,
After passing through,
These nebulous provinces,
Perhaps I have become wise and smug,
Tranquility has many forms,
We do not have to be always superior,
Or winning in every competition,
Absence and presence coexist.

April 1, 2011

Revised, first appeared in the *Who Speaks for Me?*

286　連續性

混亂是順序的一種形式,
融洽是依據參考的度數。
芳香是氣味的一部分,
對於個人的偏愛沒有明確基準。

音樂由主題及旋律組成,
它的反響與沈靜成對比。
黑色是白色光譜的一部分,
色盲者只能看見連續。

黑暗遮蓋了光明,
同樣的蒙蔽了真實與公平。
供認不完全是說事實,
允諾常常隱瞞著謊言。

投影是由一個影像而產生,
但不能沒有光源而生存。
溫暖是比熱要冷,
多少是根據人的滿足。

苦與甜是兩種極端,
混起來就造成一塌糊塗。
愛恨是在相反的兩端,
但通常的起點是相同。

2005年9月18日中秋節

　　我用「連續性」來描述兩個極端之間的灰色區域.常常兩點之間是有連接的關係, 或者一方面是依賴另一方面才能建立一個基準點。

286   **Continuity**

Chaos is a form of order,
Harmony is by a scale of reference.
Fragrance is a part of odor,
No clear indication to individuals' preference.

Music consist notes and themes,
Its resonance contrasts to silence.
Black is part spectrum of white,
Color blind can only see continuum.

Darkness obscures brightness,
Equally blinds truth and justice.
Confession is not always telling fact,
Promise often conceals fabrication.

Shadow created by an image,
It cannot exist without illumination.
Warm is colder than hot,
Measures are by personal satisfaction.

Bitter and sweet are two extremes,
Mix them together create indifference.
Love and hate are on opposite ends,
But often starts at same point.

Sept. 18, 2005 on mid-Autumn Festival

I use "Continuity" to describe the gray area of two extremes. Often there is continuous relationship between two points, or one aspect is depending on others to establish a reference.

287　春天的歡迎

經過一個惡劣的冬天，
與寒冷的冰雪，
在一個陽光溫暖的春天，
躺在柔軟的草地真是愉快非凡。

鳥在樹頭上唧唧的叫，
麻雀在樹叢裡吱吱的喊，
鄰居的女孩子們在秋千上嘻笑，
她們的父母緊緊的在旁看守。

螞蟻進進出出的忙碌，
蟋蟀在下草地裡密談。

我能聽見柔唱的風鈴，
和我自己跳著的心臟。

啄木鳥不停的敲啄樹幹，
遠遠的傳來火車的汽笛，
清柔的風溫和的太陽，
我們沉溺於不可抗拒的世界。

快樂點! 享受吧!
把握著機會。
風平浪靜的日子，
會在轉眼之間消散。

2005 年 4 月 5 日，

　　一個溫暖和平安的春天，捉住它! 沒人知道明天什麼會發生。

287 **Spring Welcome**

> After a long harsh winter,
> With freezing snow and sleet,
> Lying down on soft cool grass,
> In a sunny warm spring is a treat.
>
> Birds are chirping on tree tops,
> Sparrows tweeting in the bushes,
> Neighbor's girls giggle on the swing,
> Closely watches by their parents.
>
> Ants busy in and out their colony,
> Crickets whisper in their dens.
>
> I am listening pipes softly chime,
> And also hearing my heart thumbs.
>
> The pecking sound of a wood pecker,
> The distant whistle of a freight train,
> The soft wind and warm sun,
> We indulge in this irresistible land.
>
> Enjoy it! Be happy!
> Take whatever you can get.
> Calm days and peaceful wind,
> May vanish into thin air.
>
> April 5, 2005

What a warm and peaceful spring day. Catch it! No one knows what will happen tomorrow.

288　我們的城堡

從我的床上我看見西方的黃昏,
轉頭一瞥早晨太陽的上升,
眺望我花園和樹林的全景,
向南方的玻璃窗是為了太陽,
也讓我看所有的風景與風光。

沒有人賜給我們這些獨特的權益,
只有用我們自己的勞力及血汗。
我們為地基除清泥沙,
一石又一石,一鍬又一鍬,
從地面上建造沒什麼花梢。

建築設計與藍圖,
建立根基灌入水泥,
擱放空心磚有如水泥匠,
像木匠和電工營造外牆,
建造內在壁櫥及隔板。

它是我們的日光室與活動中心,
環圍音響的音樂廳,
電視新聞,娛樂與電影,
印表與掃描週邊設備,
電腦寫作及上網。

也許它不是你的宮廷,
但卻是我們的城堡。

2005 年六月十五日

　　此文描述我們如何修建了我們兩層新建築的整個情節。樓上是一間全能的臥室,寬裕,有風景和充分陽光。底層用來停放兩輛汽車的車房。

288   **Our Castle**

I see western twilight from my bed,
Peek at morning sunrise by turning my head,
Panorama view of my garden and woods,
Large glass window faces south for sunlight,
Also lets me to see all sceneries and sights.

No one bestowed us these unique advantages,
Only come from our own sweat and pains.
We evacuated the soil for foundation,
Stone by stone, shovel by shovel,
From ground up and nothing fancy.

Architectural plans and blue prints,
Erect footing by pouring cement,
Lay cement bricks like mason,
Building wall as if carpenter and electrician,
Construct interior partitions and closets.

It is our sunroom and center of activities,
Music hall with surrounding sound,
Television for news, movies for entertaining,
Peripheral devices for print and scan,
Computers for writing and connect to internet.

Perhaps it is not a palace for you,
But it is a castle for us.

June 15, 2005

An essay describes the entire episode and how we construct our two-level addition. It is an all-purpose upstairs bed room, spacious, full of views and sunlight. The lower level is an over sized garage, possibly for two cars.

289　門診部手術

病人在醫院的通道裡進行，
跟隨著家人的焦急，
病床排列在手術預備室，
你的生命就掛在管子和吊線。
不吉祥的時機蕭條的環境，
誰能預測你的結局與天命。

名子及生日一再的查問，
可能他們不相信你，
或許他們不相信他們自己。
醫生及護士在一旁說笑，
你像似是一種樣品，
病人僅只是標本一件。

這裡或許是最好的馬戲場，
護士們走來走去匆匆忙忙，
聽診器繞在她們的頸脖上，
皮鞋發出有節奏地刺耳聲響，
名牌掛在她們帶子或是前胸，
滿口袋裡裝的都是些東西，
車子的鑰匙、情書或者只是午餐。

預備室擠滿了醫護人員，
多數的只是不在意的聊天，
醫生說笑話護士笑的彎腰，
病人的福利不使他們煩惱。
這裡不像醫院的醫療中心，
而很像咖啡館與公共市場。

2004年六月十六日

　　門診外科手術的情節是很惶惑和困擾，也就是說，如果您從側面去看他們。

289   **Out Patience's Surgery**

　　Patients parade in hospital hallway,
　　Followed by anxious members of family,
　　Beds align in surgical preparation area,
　　Your life is hanging on the rack.
　　Ominous occasion and bleak surrounding,
　　Who can predict your fate or destiny?

　　Name and birthday were asked repeatedly,
　　Perhaps they did not believe me,
　　Or they did not believe themselves.
　　Doctors and nurses joke on the sideline,
　　As if we are some kind of dummy,
　　Patients are only a piece of specimen.

　　Here is perhaps the best circus,
　　Nurses rushing back and forth,
　　Stethoscopes wrap around their neck,
　　Rubber shoes rhythmically squeak,
　　Badges hang on their breasts or belt,
　　With something dangle fully in pockets,
　　Love letters, car keys or just lunches.

　　Preparation room is full of medical personnel,
　　Most of them just chat casually,
　　Physicians joke and nurses hilariously giggle,
　　Patients' apprehensions are not their concerns.
　　This doesn't seem like a medical center in a hospital,
　　And more resembles a coffee shop or public market.

June 16, 2004

　　The episode of an out-patient surgical procedure is both apprehensive and baffling, that is to say, if you look at it from the side line.

124   幻覺的片段

記憶像是外來的顏色，
印在我的大腦皮質，
新鮮的記憶總是生動，
時間將慢慢地腐蝕他們，
它們不可能像圖片陳列，
我卻能說明我的所作所為。
體格上我不是非常強壯，
精神上我不是那麼軟弱。

有些人認為在夢想裡他們變得機智，
或者能達成生活實際不容許可能性。
我不是浮華也不謙虛，
經驗剝奪了我的放肆。
成長在不容許講話的文化，
寢不言及食不語的閉著嘴，
枕邊細語僅是在電影的花式，
語言能力不是我喜歡喝的茶水。

那是過去而這是現在，
以財富和興旺的經濟，
傲慢帶來變形的心態，
無知和粗暴成為日用品，
有錢能買到愛和榮耀，
又有勢力能使鬼推磨。
但不知道鍾愛與尊敬非常神聖，
失敗的虎鉗總是在勝利的邊緣。

大家都假裝生活是十全十美，
經常對別人和他們自己虛偽，
保存臉面要比尊嚴和優雅重要，
有時虛擬的好像別人行為，
一個迅速發展的豐富社會的災難，
正直和誠實對貪婪讓步，
明天仍然還有一天，
今天你仍然可以欺騙。

124 Fragments of Illusion

Memory is like alien colors,
Imprinted on my cerebral cortices,
The fresh ones are always vivid,
Time will slowly erode them away.
They cannot exhibit as pictures.
I could illustrate what I do and say.
Physically I am not very macho,
Mentally I am not a wimp.

Some think they become wittier in dreams,
Or doing impossible real life prohibited,
I am neither ostentatious nor modest,
Experiences have deprived my audacity.
Brought up in a culture discouraged to speak,
Keep your mouth shut when you sleep and eat,
Pillow talks are only fancies in movies,
Linguistic ability is not my cup of tea.

That was then and this is now,
With wealth and booming economy,
Arrogance comes with distorted mentality,
Ignorance and rudeness becomes commodities,
The rich can buy love and honor,
With power to make ghosts pushing mills,
Not knowing affection and respect are sacred,
The jaw of defeat is always at the verge of victory.

Everyone pretends life is great,
Often untruthful to others and to themselves,
Saving face is more than dignity and grace,
Sometimes acting fictitiously as if someone else,
A calamity of a fast-moving material society,
Integrity and honesty yield to greed,
Tomorrow is still another day away,
Today is the day one may deceive.

291　年齡的效應

我不記得多久以前，
總是有人看守著我，
擔心我的福利，寒冷與饑餓。
他們訓戒我無聊的態度，
稱讚及獎勵我好的行為。

現在輪到我坐著悠閒，
讀我喜歡的書籍，
掃視我的樹叢與花朵，
小心的修剪它們葉子與外形。
我並不想傷害它們，
也不會無故殘殺。

年齡使你的性格軟化，
也可能失去許多身上的機敏，
或許縮短一點身高。
和降低重力的中心，
但意向並未非腐化與墮落。

你有不想動的傾向，
有較大慣性的可能，
喜歡躺下和坐在一張椅子上，
一個靜態與不靈活的象徵，
要有更多的支持與平衡，
兩隻腳變成三四隻的可能性。

你看起來也許會有點緩慢與脆弱，
別人總是認為你的思想含糊不明。
如果他們找不到藉口，
總是會有為難的時間，
最後高舉他們的雙手，
帶著令人作嘔的手勢離去。

　　攤開他們的雙手作一個令人作嘔的姿態揚長而去的人，
或許從未瞭解年老的優雅是自然贈送的禮物。

291   **Aging**

    I do not remember how long ago,
    Someone always watches over me;
    Care for my welfare, cold and hungry.
    They discipline my poor behaviors,
    Praise and reward my good deeds.

    It is now my turn to sit in my leisure,
    Read whatever soothes me,
    Glance over my bushes and flowers,
    Tenderly manicure their shapes and leaves.
    I do not wish to harm them,
    Nor mutilate them without reason.

    Age makes you soft in character,
    You lose a lot of physical agility,
    Perhaps height, shortening a bit,
    And lower the center of gravity;
    But mind is not necessarily degenerated.

    You have the tendency to stay put,
    Apt to have larger moment of inertia,
    Prefer lying down and sitting in a chair;
    A symptom of static and non mobile ,
    To get more support and stability,
    Two legs may become three or four.

    You may look a bit slow and frail,
    People always think your mind is cloudy.
    If they don't find excuse to say so,
    There is always a moment of perplexity.
    In the end, throw their hands up in the air,
    Walk away with a disgusted gesture.

    People who throw their hands up and walk away with a disgusted gesture perhaps never understood the grace of age is a gift of nature.

292　國慶日的極端

多麼一批大雜燴的人群，
從世界每一個角落收集而成，
他們主要的目標是為更好的生活，
慶祝七月四日國慶享受煙火，
熱狗填滿他們肥胖的腸胃，
但並不關心它真正的意義。

人權保護他們平等，
法律保護他們免受歧視，
崇拜他們的宗教和傳統，
又幾乎不會講幾句英文，
不但不愛護這片國土，
有些圖謀殺害我們的子孫。

由以汽車製造的優勢惡化，
白種人仍然買美國產品，
歐洲人總是傾向德國貨，
然後是那些實際的亞洲人，
購買日本汽車和電子，
貪心的買那些便宜中國產品。

自由和自由言論可能買得通，
窮人非法地偷渡邊界，
富商們用錢買他們的入境證，
政治或宗教家請求政治庇護，
船民們前來如同一群難民，
專家們卻以特權而被邀請。

2005 年 7 月 4 日美國慶日

在 9-11 之後，我無法忽略我們每日有刺激性的一些極端發生。過失不是歸因於任何人而是對許多自由權利的濫用。

292   **Independents Day Extreme**

What a group of hodgepodge people,
Collected from every corner of the world,
Their major goals are for better living,
Celebrating 4th of July enjoying fireworks,
Stuffing hot dogs in their fat bellies,
But care not about its real meaning.

Human rights guarantee them equality,
Laws protect them from discrimination,
Worship their heritages and religions,
And barely speak a few words of English,
Rather than patriotic to this land,
Some of them plot to kill our offspring.

With deteriorating superiority in car-making,
Caucasians still buy American products,
Europeans always favor those made in Germany,
Then there are practical Asians,
Buy Japanese cars and electronics,
And devour cheap goods from China.

Freedom and free speech can be bought,
Poor people illegally sneak in from borders,
Wealthy businessmen buy their entries,
Political or religious individual claims asylum,
Boat people come as a group of refugees,
Specialists are invited to come with privileges.

July 4, 2005

After 9-11, I cannot help to think some of the extreme occurrences that haunt our day-to-day life. The fault is not attributed to any individual, but to the abuse of too many rights and privileges.

293　老貓

一棟房子和兩個老人,
又有兩隻來訪的老貓,
動物們一年一度的渡假,
那些可憐的居民未能得到救助。

過去十年來每年的慣例,
籠子、領圈、食料及貓的方便沙粒,
最近又新增加了醫藥的須要,
給貓的特別食物和處方,
醫治發炎的抗生素和甲狀腺。

更不要提人的醫藥責任,
治療骨質疏鬆的佛斯梅,
和肩膀發腫的止痛藥片,
鍛煉肌肉的配件和用具,
按摩椅子解除日常的疲倦。

房子裡充滿了活動,
你去那裡它們跟你到那裡,
有佔領您喜歡椅子的優先,
通常都睡在你的枕頭邊,
大聲打鼾鼻子顫動。

凡事都有恩惠也有缺點,
貓毛使你的眼鼻發癢,
大小便的氣味臭薰你的房間,
他們的感情也許是懇切和真實,
目的是希望回報它們好吃的東西。

2005 年 7 月 8 日

因為*海綿*的肩膀有大手術,*軟豆糖*患有甲狀腺症,所以她們今年都要有特別照料。這次來訪之後不久,它們兩者都死於老年。

293   **Old Cats**

A house has two old folks,
Coming visiting by two aged cats,
Annual vacation for these animals,
Those poor residents don't get any relief.

Yearly practice for the last decade,
Cages, collars, foods and cat litters,
Lately new remedies are added,
Prescriptions and special diets for cats,
Antibiotics for infection and thyroid pills.

Not to mention people's medical obligations,
Fosamax for osteoporosis of bones,
Ibuprofen relieves shoulder inflammation.
Gadgets and gears for muscle exercise,
Massage chair relieves the daily fatigues

This house fills with activities,
They follow you everywhere you go,
Occupy your favorite spot of a chair,
Normally sleep beside your pillow,
Snore loudly with vibrating noise.

There are drawbacks and also rewards,
Cats' hairs make your nose and eyes itch,
Smell of litters fumigate your rooms,
Their affections may be sincere and genuine,
To a point they wish to have a treat in return.

July 8, 2005

Special cares were needed this year due to a major surgery on Sponge's shoulder and thyroidal treatment for Jelly-bean. Both cats died no long after this visit.

294 大易的不易

啊!卡瓊娜,多迷人的名字,
它不是傳奇故事裡的幻想,
而是殘忍的與無情的現實,
在面紗及薄霧之後,
帶來的是殘忍的威脅及危險。

所有的號召與警報沒人理睬,
鵬駕船湖擴大了它的範圍,
河堤及水壩對暴力而投降,
街道淹沒的有如運河,
建築物翱翔相似海市蜃樓。

我看見淒慘的臉和失望的表情,
我看見絕望老弱的市民,
我看見許多在屋頂上揮動的手,
我看見官員們傲慢的無能,
我看見官僚們躊躇與不關心。

如果颶風沒有摧殘他們的希望,
洪水無疑的展示它的威力,
大火與火焰增加它們的憤怒,
一個城市浸在水中有如湖泊,
而有人號稱無水消滅火焰。

火災數吋之外就是洪水,
但是沒有機智也是很遠,
救火船及抽水機的發明,
只是別人的想像,
新奧爾良市也許是例外。

2005 年 8 月 30 日

　　颶風卡瓊娜展示她的威力,政府和城市機構也同樣的展示他們的無能。可憐的人民就夾在當中。

294   Uneasy in the Big Easy

O! Katrina, what a charming name,
It is not a fantasy of fairy tales,
But brutal and cruel reality,
Behind the veil and the mist,
Coming tragically with the menace.

All alerts and warnings went unnoticed,
Lake Pontchartrain extended its domain,
Levees and dams yielded to power of demand,
Streets flooded deep as canals,
Buildings hovered like mirages in the sea.

I see the sad faces and desperate expressions,
I see the hopeless old and weak citizens,
I see many hands waving about the roof,
I see the pathetic act of officials' arrogances,
I see bureaucratic hesitations and indifferences.

If hurricane does not destroy their hope,
Flood certainly displays its potency,
And fire and blaze add to their furies.
A city submerged in flood looks like a lake,
People claim no water to put out the flames.

Fires are inches away from flooded water,
Yet too far to be useful without ingenuity,
The invention of fire boats and pumps,
Only for someone else's imagination,
New Orleans perhaps is exceptional.

Aug 30, 2005

Hurricane Katrina certainly demonstrates her power; similarly, government and city agencies also demonstrate their power of inability. The poor folks are the only ones caught in between.

295　泥和尚過河

早晨從我溫柔舒適的床，
我聽見匆忙的交通，
我既不羨慕他們的行為，
也不煩惱他們的舉動。

在不久之前和最近的過去，
我像他們一樣如一隻螞蟻，
為生存，
富裕與名望而戰爭，
或者只是為了自我與光榮。

我現時坐在籬笆的另一邊，
毫無興趣的，
在線外旁觀，
在現實中無論為何原因，
掙扎將會繼續。

在我窗外的道路，
是公共的領域，
惱怒的嘈雜侵犯了我的範圍，
我是否對他們的奔波有所同情，
或只是我非常羞恥，
未能給於一點憐憫。

為什麼我們要關心，
那些幽靈的事務？
別人一點也不注意，
我們都像泥和尚
過河，
自身難保。

　　我站在旁邊觀看人群精神振奮的奮鬥。我毫無興趣去擔心他們做什麼。每人都是自掃門前雪，那管他人瓦上霜。

295   **Clay Monks Crossing Rive**

From my soft and comfortable bed,
I hear the rushing traffic in the morning,
I neither envy their movements,
Nor annoy their actions.

Not so long ago and recent past,
I am one of them like matching ants;
Battle for survival,
For rich and for fame,
Or just for selfishness and glory.

I am now sitting on the other side of fence,
With benign interest,
Watching from the sideline,
For whatever reasons in reality,
The struggle will continue.

The road outside my window
is a public realm,
Noise has exasperated invading my domain,
Should I be sympathetic for their rushing?
Or just being very shameful of myself,
For not taking any pity.

Why should we concern,
Those ghostly affairs?
No one has paid any attention.
We are all like clay monks
crossing the river,
Dangerously being dissolved by the stream.

I stand on the sideline watching crowd vigorously struggle. I have little interest to worry what they are fighting about. Everyone only shovels snow in front of their door and not worry the frost on others roof.

301　公民權

在這個行星上和空氣中，
光線把我們投射成暫時陰影，
吹風給我們帶來新鮮的空氣，
雨水洗去我們的污染。
我們在這個球面上不停的忙碌，
倉促的有如沒有明天。

我們測量太陽的高度，
觀看月亮盈虧的演變，
才能告訴我們什麼時間午餐，
我們無窮盡的奔波去捕捉幻影，
來滿足我們的自私自利；
一天結尾仍未滿意。

在生死之間短暫的片刻，
與宇宙的年齡相比，無窮盡，
我們的生命相似擦一根火柴，
只有片刻的照明，
然後又突然間的熄滅，
偶然的事件又變得沒有事件。

當地球在太空裡奔馳，
完全由物理的理論而統治，
我們只是在遼闊領域裡的碎片，
對地球的演化沒有半點關連，
我們既不能改變它的軌道或運動，
只能移動我們自己是由於它的運行。

我們都是為個人設想的生物，
對此行星毫無貢獻，
污染它的土壤與海洋，
毒害人的精神及心情，
我們善於浪費和虛張聲勢，
包括消耗它可貴的氧氣。

301 **Rights of Citizenship**

On this planet and in this air,
Light casts us into temporary shadow,
Wind brings us circulation and freshness,
And rain washes off our contamination.
We busy restlessly on this globe,
Hurry on as if there is no tomorrow.

We measure the height of sun,
And watch the changing phases of moon,
In order to tell us when to have lunch,
We rush endlessly to catch illusion,
To please our ego and selfishness;
Still aren't satisfied at the end of day.

Between birth and death, a short span,
To the age of cosmos, infinite;
Our life resembles striking a match,
For a little while of brilliances,
Then extinguished instantaneously,
The event is becoming non event.

While the earth is dashing in space,
Dominated by the laws of physics,
We are only a dust speck in the vast realm,
Inconsequential to its evolution,
We can neither change its orbit nor motion,
Only move ourselves by its movement.

We are all self-serving organisms,
Contribute nothing to this planet,
Pollute its soil and ocean,
And poison people's mind and emotion,
We are good for waste and extravagant,
Include consuming its valuable oxygen.

整個的行星喪失光澤，
充滿了疾病與戰爭，
在這裡，我不停的掃除和清洗，
希望能保護一小塊的地面，
少一點粗俗及多一點神聖，
為我做公民一點微小的貢獻。

2005 年 10 月 10 日

　　我不希望給您印象，我是唯一在這個行星上的公民保護它的正直。我同樣的像所有的人呼吸氧氣和消費資源，但只是限制在我個人的範圍而不影響到他人。

The entire planet tarnishes with pollution,
And fills with wars and diseases,
Here, I am mopping and washing,
Hope to preserve a small piece of earth,
Less vulgar and more sacred,
Offering a tiny payment for my citizenship.

Oct. 10, 2005

I do not wish to give you impression that I am the only citizen on this planet to protect its integrity. I breathe oxygen and exhaust resources just like everyone, but limited to my single entity and not affect anyone else.

307　大器晚成者

我看見他們，淘金者，
佈置他們機會的帳篷，
在集會中講得非常出色，
用一些虛構的托辭，
擴展他們捏造的羅網。
我只是一個普通的實行人，
他們不會給我多少機會，
在湖裡捕獲任何大魚。

我是一個沒有經驗的漁夫，
坐在急速河流旁邊，
和一個空而焦急的魚網，
與滿罐誘餌的渴望，
能抓到幾個慢遊的展望，
來滿足一個老人的幻想。

咳!你們那些追求命運的人，
在這裡排隊，那邊是開始，
我是你們其中之一，晚成者，
總是在節拍的幾步之後，
當我們趕上他們的步驟，
或許只留下沙塵讓我們捕捉。

假如你在我的前面，
不要回頭或向我招手，
也不要說風涼話或瞪眼，
體諒我從那裡來，
我已經在許多人的前面，
沒有吞下太多的憐憫。

2008 年 10 月 16 日

　　一個現實的估計來評價我自己的經驗和困境，然而又充分地明白潮流在我附近沖洗。

307   A Late Bloomer

I have seen them, the gold diggers,
Setting up their tents of opportunities,
Speaking elegantly in gatherings and parties,
With alibis of fictitious advantages,
And spreading their net of fabrications,
I am a plain doer with modest skill,
They do not give me the light of day,
Catch any big fish in the lake.

I am an inexperienced fisherman,
Sitting by the fast moving current of chance,
With an emptied net of anxiety,
And a full can of bait in desires,
Trying to seize a few slow moving prospects,
To fulfill an old man's reverie.

Hey! All you destiny seekers,
Here is the line, there is the beginning,
I am one of you, a late bloomer.
Always a few steps behind the beat,
By the time we caught the pace.
Perhaps only dust left for us to catch.

If you are in front of me,
Do not look back or wave,
Nor stare or speak your insult,
Considering where I came from,
I am already ahead of many others,
And not gulping down too much pity.

Oct 16, 2008

A realistic appraisal assessing my own experiences and predicament, yet fully aware the current washes around me.

504 晚春片語

陽光使萬物穿上顏色,
又使大家在晚上披上黑紗。
當我們在黑暗中酣睡的時候,
地球的另一邊是五顏六色與活潑。
如果整個地球都是神志清楚與蘇醒,
地球大概是非常喧鬧和厭煩。

太陽製造雲彩與風雨,
又在夏季創作彩虹。
我們不可能用它作為行駛的橋梁,
也不可以在彩虹的拱門下甜睡,
我們不值得如此的被尊敬;
那是給想像的專用與崇拜者。

太陽是一位仁慈和慷慨的供給者,
地球是一位公正及明智的去分配。
我們不是同時做同一件事,
一處多雲其他的地方晴朗,
在下午把風造成迅速與煩躁,
在晚上鎮靜的使性情冷下來。

當我們在睡覺或勞動的時候,
太陽已經移動了成千上萬哩,
生命連續的誕生或死亡。
地球自轉一周我已看夠了一切,
只是渴望溫暖的春天和熱的夏季,
和五顏六色的秋景和冬天白雪。

2008 年 5 月 28 日

504   Gabbles in Late Spring

The sun dresses everything in color,
And makes everyone wear black at night,
While we soundly sleep in darkness,
Others side of the earth were colorful and alive.
If the entire earth is awake and conscious,
It would be probably very noisy and restless.

The sun creates clouds and rains,
And makes rainbows in the summer,
We can never use it as a bridge for travel,
Nor have the privilege to sleep under its arch,
We are not worthy enough to be honored;
That is reserved for imagination and fantasy.

The sun is a gracious and generous provider,
And the earth is a wise distributor.
It is not a coincident we have different seasons,
Or cloudy in one place and sunny in another,
As wind becomes agitating in the afternoon,
But calmly cools down the temper at night.

While we sleep or labor ourselves,
Earth has traveled millions of miles,
Lives are born or die continuously.
I see enough activities in one earth rotation,
Just longing for warm spring and hot summer,
And colorful autumn and winter white.

May 28, 2008

507 無作為症狀

世界上有實行家和旁觀者，
實行者衝破他們的頭腦做事，
旁觀者則等待您犯過錯，
由於不良的因素或是好的起因，
是為一樣事件太多或是太少，
批評來自一切行動範圍之內，
怨言和稱讚有助於確實性的改造。

在劇院有演員和觀眾，
演奏者表演管理者執行，
演員和觀眾在劇終後分散，
在人潮波浪中推擠向前，
歡樂、慶祝和享受榮耀，
經理們和道具設計師留守在後，
清掃及計劃下一幕的情節。

真正的英雄是在前線爬，
或被路旁炸彈爆炸與面對狙擊手，
將軍們在戰壕裡不關心的執行命令，
愚蠢的政客在辦公室裡隱藏。
他們只計數他們獲得了多少獎章，
饒舌者撕掉您的尊嚴和禮儀；
騙子們則掃除你銀行帳戶與財產。

這是一個自我促進的社會，
助長他們自己第一其他的活該，
新聞界只關心瘋狂和荒唐事件，
機會主義者則利用他們發財，
如果您富有，有勢力或有名望，
不適當的行為是可以寬讓，
它也許甚而變得流行及時尚。

2007年6月

507   **Benign Syndrome**

There are doers and spectators in this world,
Doers beat their heads to make things work,
Bystanders wait for you to make a mistake,
For a bad reason or for a good cause,
For too many of one thing or too few else,
Criticism comes with the territory;
Complaint and praise improve validity.

There are actors and audiences in a theater,
Performers perform and stage handlers handle,
Players and watchers walk away after the show,
To ride in the front of the wave of pageantry,
Festivity, celebration and enjoy glory,
Managers and prop designers stay behind,
Clean-up and plan for the next episode.

The real heroes crawl in the front line,
Blowup by the roadside bombs and snipers,
Generals carry-out orders indifferently in bunkers,
Thick-headed politicians hide in offices.
They count only how many medals they have won
Rappers rip-off your civility and dignity;
Scammers wipe out your bank account and asset.

This is a self-promoted society of people,
Help themselves first and too bad for others.
Media care only the frenzy and trash news,
And opportunists use them to make profits.
If you are rich, fame, influential or powerful,
Inappropriate behaviors are justifiable,
It might even become trendy and fashionable.

June 2007

538 被動的反應

當楓葉變紅，
門前裝飾著南瓜，
菊花開始盛開，
一個新的季節即將來臨。
不論您準備好了還是沒有，
清理煙囪與掃耙落葉已經是時間。

我就像班車上的大輪子，
與時間變化不斷的轉動。
服從跟隨季節的風雨，
我們的行動是相當被動與微弱，
年年的變動不是真正的自願；
無形的皮鞭總是在旁邊。

但是，我們總是抵制自然，
用傘及天篷遮蔽陽光，
我們剝得赤裸避免炎熱，
或躲在有空調的室內，
穿著厚重的外套躲避寒風；
冬天在冰雪上撒沙子和鹽，
修造隄堰防衛洪水氾濫，
我們叫他們為明智的妨礙。

然而，我們幾乎不能防護人的惡習，
被欺騙時表達我們的不滿，
虐待的時候抗議屈辱，
遭受違犯保護我們的尊嚴，
哀傷時我們不可能公開哭泣，
當感情充溢的時候大聲笑。
我們唯一能出氣的是對天空詛咒，
禮義使我們表現得像人。

2008 你 9 月 22 日

538   **Passive Reaction**

When maple leaves turn red,
Doorsteps are decorated with pumpkins,
And chrysanthemums begin to blossom,
A new season is just around the corner.
Whether you are ready or not,
It is time to clean the chimney and rake leaves.

We are all like big wheels on a wagon,
Turning with the ever changing time,
Obediently follow the season,
Our actions are rather passive and meek,
Yearly variation is not truly voluntary;
After all, the invisible whip is always near.

We are always against Nature,
Shade sunlight with umbrella or canopy,
Strip naked to avoid boiling heat,
Or hide indoor with air-conditioning,
We wrap ourselves to shelter cold.
Spread sand on sleet in winter,
And build dikes to fend flooding;
We call them intelligent preventions.

Yet, we can hardly defend human abuses,
Express our dissatisfaction when deceived,
Protest humiliation when subjected ill treatment,
Protect our dignity when violated.
We can't cry openly when sad,
Laugh loudly when exuberant.
Curse to the sky is our only outlet,
Good manners make us to behave like a man.

Sept. 22, 2008

541　分享空間

太平的鄰近寂靜的空氣，
棕色的草葉多日無雨；
易碎的葉子彌漫乾燥的氣味。
螞蟻倉促地搜尋蟋蟀潺潺的私語，
我的世界雖小但又十分有餘，
我們幸運的分享這一點空間。

秋天下落的樹葉在空中飛舞，
偶爾的輕輕擦過和撫摩我的臉，
它們是否來自友善？
或是向下方飄落並非自願。
為什麼我要關心它們真正的企圖？
我應該感到幸喜和他們相遇。

我希望這是個偶然無辜的接觸，
沒有骯髒的態度和惡劣的目的，
我們之後將會忘記這個場合，
沒有懊惱的激怒或之後的苦澀。
螞蟻在我的胳膊爬行沒有惡意，
而昆蟲私語是他們神聖的賦予。

明亮的陽光充溢了我整個房間，
蒙昧了我的眼睛削減了我的意識。
在窗臺上的秋海棠十分歡喜，
為了它們的快樂我壓制我的不如意。
我們渴望被愛需要養料才能興旺，
吸收陽光是植物自然的習慣。

2007 年 10 月 6 日

541   **Sharing Space**

Peaceful neighborhood calm air,
Brittle leaves permeate with crispy dry smell,
Sky crisscrossed with south flying geese,
Ants search hastily and crickets murmur.
My world is small but with lots to spare,
We are fortunate to share this little space.

Falling leaves dance in the autumn air,
Occasionally graze and caress my face,
Are they coming as a friendly gesture?
Or just cascading involuntarily downward,
Why should I care about their real aims?
I should be blessed for the encounter.

I hope it is an innocent and casual contact,
No vicious objective and no foul attitude,
We will forget the occasion afterwards,
No annoyed irritation or bitter aftertastes.
Ant crawls on my arm has no hostile intent,
And insect murmurs are their holy heritage.

Bright sunlight floods my entire room,
Blinds my eyes and curtail my awareness.
Begonias on the windowsill love it,
I subdue my displeasure for their happiness.
We thirst for love and need nourishment to thrive,
Plants soak in sunlight as their natural habit

Oct. 6, 2007

549　自然狀態

今晚，夜更加黑暗，
然後黑夜轉向黎明。
今晨，天變得輝煌燦爛，
一點點曙光及少許拂曉，
一切改變，什麼都未曾改變;
黑暗和光亮相互要求歸還。

黑暗是黑暗，光明是光明，
之間我們看見虹的彩色與朦朧，
沒有人關心它們的意義和詳情。
即使時間在引力場也微弱的變動。
沒有太陽和沒有光明及黑暗;
時間沒有意義季節失掉卓越。

沒有歷史和沒有日曆，
昨天，明天，在一年之內，
在幾個世紀或百萬年，
誰能說日與日及年與年?
我們使它配合我們每日的生活，
在我們居住的地方當地球旋轉。

或許黑暗是在它永恆的形式，
在空隙間，在世界的終點，
既使光亮也被黑暗吞沒，
萬物回到它自然的狀態。
沒有基準、沒有霸權也無混亂。

2008 年 10 月 31 日

549   **Natural State**

This evening, night grows darker,
Then nighttime turns to daybreak.
This morning, the day becomes brilliant,
A little bit of twilight and not much dawn,
Everything changes yet nothing changes;
Darkness and brightness mutually reclaim.

Dark is dark and bright is bright,
In between, we see color of rainbow and gloom,
No one cares their significances and details,
In the gravitational field, even time faintly varies.
Without sun and without light and darkness,
Time has no meaning and seasons lose prominence.

Without history and without a calendar,
Yesterday, tomorrow and in one year,
In a few centuries or hundreds of millennia,
Who can tell day to day and year to year?
We make it to fit our own daily purposes,
In where we reside and as the earth rotates.

Perhaps darkness is in its perpetual form,
In a region of void or at the end of the world,
Even brightness is swallowed up by the darkness,
Everything returns to its natural state,
No reference, no domination and no chaos.

Oct. 31, 2008 Halloween

555　我們的世界與生活

我們的世界是充滿了燦爛的顏色，
我們經常看他們是黑與白。
我們的生活通常是暗淡較少華麗，
我們可以使它五顏六色與光彩。

生命的宗旨是搜索快樂，
以一點想像生命可以充滿活力，
以一點奇異世界可以是美麗。
自然愛好是力量的來源，
品德的賢良是起自以神志清醒。

啟發是自製，好像山崖的溫泉，
生命的激勵是興趣和熱心，
意志和熱誠是促進者，
經驗和教養是智慧。
它來自大腦最深外皮和根莖；
而不是攝取物質或興奮劑。

我的世界充滿著音樂和詩詞，
書是為充實，音樂是為渴望，
我在您的視域之下可能是天使，
但在我的情緒裡可能是一個魔王。

沒有人領導我或設置路線，
我是我自己的領航員和船長，
單獨操縱我的舵輪去到命運的終點。

2008 年 11 月 20 日

555   **Our World and Our Life**

Our world is full of dazzling colors,
We often see them black and white.
Our life is normally dull with less sparkle,
We could make it colorful and splendid.

The objective of life is searching for happiness,
Life can be lively with a bit of imagination,
The world can be wonderful with a bit of wondering.
The love of nature is the source of strength,
The conscience of virtue is from consciousness.

Inspiration is self-made as a mountain spring,
The stimulation is the zest of life and passion,
Determination and enthusiasm are the motivators,
Experience and learning from life is wisdom.
It comes from the inner layer of the cortex;
Not the intake of stimulant or substances.

My world fills with music and poetry,
Books for thirst and music for enrichment,
I could be an angel in your view,
But I can be a devil in my sentiment.

No one leads me or lays me a course,
I am my own pilot and captain,
To my destiny, I steer the helm alone.

Nov. 20, 2008

568　無止境的掙扎

新年現在已變得舊年，
新年的決定已失去意義。
我們又爬回到我們的角落，
再開始爭先恐後的掙扎，
為生存和繁榮而交戰，
或尋找我們失去已久的含糊光榮。

我認為我已經與那些奔波無關，
埋在我自造的孤立，
在音樂、在讀書、在詩詞之間，
為可憐的獎勵而搏鬥已失去光輝，
騷亂的世界像煙火一樣的遙遠，
我以為那是在我日程裡的慣例。

我就像我平常仍是匆匆忙忙，
相信那裡有一座光彩的城堡，
它從未存在也未必是如然，
我自己創作許諾的堡壘，
只是解除臨時性的熱情洋溢，
雖然我並不尋求英名及利益。

我晚間上床仍然充滿了憂慮，
每天醒了之後又有新的活力，
它好像是從精神的壓力機榨出，
助長我的信念我可以隨心所欲，
我只是在彙聚枯萎的花瓣，
再去創造不可能實現幻覺的花朵。

2008 年 1 月 6 日

568   **Never Ending Struggle**

Now the New Year is becoming old,
The fresh resolutions have vanished.
We are all crawling back to our corners,
Scrambling for our usual daily struggle,
Battling for our own survival and prosperity,
Or searching for our long-lost hazy glory.

I thought I was removed from the rush,
Embedded in my self-made solitude,
In music, in reading and in poetry,
Wrestling for the pitiful reward has faded,
The frenzied world is as remote as fireworks,
That was what I thought in my itinerary.

I am scuttling about like me as usual,
In the belief that there is a glorious citadel,
The promised fortress is my own manufacture,
It neither ever once was nor ever will be,
Though what I seek is not rich or eminence,
Only to quench the temporary eagerness.

Yet I went to bed late in full of apprehensions,
And woke up each day with a new vitality,
It seems squeezing out from a mental press,
With the belief that I could still be very witty,
I was just gathering flakes of the wilted flowers,
Trying to recreate a blossom that never could be.

Jan. 6, 2008

569　無從捉摸的命運

我是一個貧困鄉村年青人,
注定是一個勇敢和反叛的男孩,
光著屁股和赤腳來到這個世界,
我不預定是一位鄉村的農民,
在泥濘的田裡弄得渾身是泥,
牛犁、鏟子和鐮刀不是我的工具。

其餘是完全靠我的耐力,
許多的失敗和少許的運氣。
不知道日出或日落,
雲彩造雨和寒冷製造冰雨,
在我頭上滿天是旋轉與揮動星星,
我無教養的像一頭水牛或毛驢。

我夢想做一個有技能的工程師,
只學會引導炮兵練習打靶的哨兵,
那是我做工程師最可能的接近。
命運帶著我在公海上流浪,
或在山峰上偵察宇宙的奧秘,
我的發現幾乎不值得浪費我的睡眠。

我從落寞孩兒的命運裡逃脫,
但不能從我的命運中逃避,
臉面老化前景變遷,
在一個遙遠的國度說奇怪的言語,
搜尋生命中無從捉摸的真理;
地平線上的視野仍是荒涼一片。

2008年1月8日

569   **Elusive Fate**

I was an underprivileged country youth,
Destined to be a valiant and rebellious boy,
Came with a naked bottom and two bare feet,
I was not meant to be a rural farmer,
Sloshing in the field with muddy hands and knees,
Ploughs, spades and sickles were not my gear.

The rest is entirely up to my endurance,
A little bit of luck and a lot of defeats.
Knowing nothing about sunrise or sunset,
Clouds make rain and cold rain makes sleet,
Starry sky above my head twirling and swishing,
I was ill-bred and dumb as a buffalo or donkey.

I dreamt to be an engineer with adamant skills,
Only learned to guide target practice in artillery,
The closest to be an engineer I can ever be.
Destiny led me tramping in the open sea,
Scouting the universe on the mountain peaks,
What I found is hardly worthy of wasting my sleep.

I ran away from my desolate childhood,
But could not escape from my own destiny,
The landscape has changed and face aged,
In a distant land spoke strange language,
Searching for the elusive truth of life;
The view on the horizon is still bleak

Jan. 8, 2008

572　最終的贖罪

以人類的知識，
我們多數都沒有特權，
在出生時我們有相等的天賦，
沒有人比不重要更重要，
沒有人比不值得更值得。

我們裸露及無牙齒的出生，
有個頭腦和類似的無知，
強健的人勇敢的力爭上游，
靈巧的人能遠看比岸，
軟弱的人隨著河水向下流，
最後變得平平常常。

或許那就是人的不同，
在種族，在家庭地位與在地理，
一些為生存而去洗刷桶底，
一些做首腦，其他的做民眾，
有些人指責備家庭其他責備命運，
一命抵一命，一體對一體，
為什麼我們應該為他人擔當責備？

聖人負擔他自己的缺點，
狡猾的那些讓別人承受他們的責任。
當我們全都在努力的保守我們的崗位，
他們卻在圓球面上移動尋找展望，
認為他們越來越靠近他的目標，
但實際卻接近他的起點。
一個既無覺悟又不慎重的人，
隨風飄蕩應該是得到的命運。

生命的每件事都有無條文的束縛，
家庭生活及婚姻的責任，
愛護寵畜與關心環境，
清除落葉以及保持庭院整潔，
對我們的職業和工作熱誠，
國家忠誠與尊敬自己，
我們的行為顯示我們品格，
我們生存最終的贖罪，
是決定我們的文明態度及尊嚴。

572 **Ultimate Redemption**

With the knowledge of human species,
I see most of us are underprivileged,
We all had equal gifts at birth,
No one is more important or unimportant,
More worthy or less worthy.

We were born naked and toothless,
With one brain and similar ignorance,
The courageous ones strive for upstream,
The clever ones can see the distant land,
And the weak bunch flow down the river,
Ending up in the ocean of mediocrity.

Perhaps this is normal among people,
In race, family status and geography,
Some scrub the bottom of the barrel for survival,
A few become chiefs and others the hoi polloi,
Some blame fate and others accuse family,
One life to one life and one body to one body,
Why should we bear other's culpability?

Wise man shoulders his own fault,
Devious ones let others carry their guilt.
While we are diligently defending our post,
They are wandering on a round globe,
Thinking they are approaching their goal,
But actually moving closer to their origin.
A man who is neither sensible nor prudent,
Deserving the fate of fluttering in the wind.

Everything in life has an unwritten bond,
The responsibility of family life and marriage,
Caring for our pets and respecting environment,
Raking leaves and keeping yards tidy.
We devoted to our profession and duty,
Loyal to our country and respect ourselves.
What we do or act displaying our character,
The ultimate redemption of our existence,
Determining our civility and sanctity.

574 預誠

我看見自己橫跨在一個洞口，
去到來世黑暗深遠的隧道，
以我的四肢寬闊伸展到它的外緣，
堅強的為懸浮而掙扎。

我看不見在我附近以外的範圍，
只有想到落入空虛後的結尾。
放鬆我的掌握之後就無回歸，
或許那是死亡真正的滋味。

生存的理由非常稀薄與膚淺，
我沒有看見坑底有任何光線，
只有面對虛無和靜寂，
我醒過來發現我正在睡眠。

我不知道哪張床和我睡的地方，
在我自己的世界或在幻想，
或是漂泊在一個夢中的夢鄉，
我爬起來證實我是在哪世界。

我看見我大門前的來回腳印，
門鈴沈默郵箱空閒。
使者沒有給我留下資訊，
徵收的天使決定饒我一命。

在我們自己的世界我沒有妄想，
雅致的結束老年是特權。
我們忍受一生已經是夠長，
空曠與沈寂或許是平安。

2008 年 1 月 28 日

574 **Premonition**

I see myself flatly extended across a pit,
Above a dark and deep tunnel to eternity,
With my limbs stretch widely to hold on its rim,
Vigorously struggles for levitation.

I cannot see beyond my immediate surroundings,
Only think the outcome of falling into emptiness
There will be no return after I let go my grip,
Perhaps that is the real taste of death.

Raison d'être is so thin and shallow
I see no light from the bottom of the hollow,
Only nothingness and soundless that facing me,
I woke up to find that I am only in sleep.

I did not know where and what bed I lay,
In my own world or in a fantasy,
Or drifted in a dream of dreams,
I get up to validate which world I am in.

I saw footprints leading to my front door,
Door bell was silent and mail box empty.
The messenger left me with no messages,
The angel of collector decided to let me live.

I have no illusion in our own world,
Dying old gracefully is privilege,
One life is long enough for us to endure,
Emptiness and silence is perhaps peace.

Jan. 28, 2008

575　春季的熱潮預誡 (俳句詩)

冬天將完結，
季節變換像鐘錶，
如我們心跳。

一次是一秒，
太陽返回舊榮耀，
春來玩花招。

林園再復活，
樹枝佩帶著綠梢，
葉子自芽來。

花開成花朵，
由它們自己安排，
不是我感慨。

要享受春意，
您必須品嘗嚴寒，
那有是免費。

時間很公平，
一路鏟平人行道，
我們像是草。

在路的末端，
塵對塵灰回到灰，
生命是循環，
年輕再生又變老，
我們爬起又跌倒。

2008年1月31日

575   **Spring Fever (Haiku)**

Winter will soon end,
Season change like clocks tick,
Same as our heart beat.

One second a time,
Sun returns with old glory,
Spring hype is near.

Life revives in woods,
Tree branches carry green tips,
Buds sprout in to leaves.

Flowers start to bloom,
By their own time and schedule,
Not by my pleasure,

To enjoy spring breeze,
You have to taste the cruel freeze,
Nothing is ever free.

Time very fair,
Swaths everything in its path,
We are as if grass.

At the end of road,
Ash to ash and dust to dust,
Life is in cycles,
Young become old then reborn,
We rise then fall down again。

Jan. 31, 2008

576　隱喻

我們全來自某處，
又倉促的去到別的地方，
我們今天能去那裡和多遠，
全要看我們，
過去的栽培。

跟隨別人的腳步相當容易，
但很難有您自己遠景與先見，
我只是位尋找啟發可憐的獵手，
散佈預言不是我的專業。

我尋找一條有利小道，
橫渡繁榮荒涼的領域，
我沒有發現大道和小徑，
面對著我是蕭條一片，
生命的歷程仍須繼續。

星圖也許提供某人指南，
我知道他們不是我的天命。
生命的跡象也許帶領我的去向，
我不能信任他們的正直或真實性。

我既沒有假定又沒有優先，
前進去任何方向都是進展。
去到某處或世界的末端，
靜止不是選擇，
而是一事無成。

我們沒有多少選擇做最終的決定，
沒有預測，沒有期望與無後悔，
當情況和選擇並不明確，
讓希望和機會決定我將來命運。

2008年2月4日

576   Metaphor

We are all coming from somewhere,
And hastily going somewhere else,
How far and where we can go today,
Depends upon our cultivation
from past years.

It is effortless to follow others' footsteps,
But difficult to foresee your own prospect,
I am only a poor hunter for inspiration,
Spreading prophecy is not my specialty.

I was looking for an advantageous trail,
To cross the bleak field of prosperity,
I found neither avenue nor track,
Everything facing me was desolate.
Journey of life needs to proceed.

Star charts may offer someone a guide,
I have known they are not my destiny.
Signs of life may lead me the way,
I can't trust their authenticity or integrity.

I have neither hypotheses nor preferences,
Advancing in any direction is progress,
To somewhere or to the end of the world,
Stationary is defeat-
Not an alternative.

We make the final decision with little choice,
No divination, no expectation and no regret.
Even circumstances and options are vague,
Let opportunity and possibility be my fate.

Feb. 4, 2008

二. 生命的透視

我覺得自己與樹上的葉子沒有不同，
經驗循環茂盛和死亡的命運，
只是我並不如小植物那樣的應變，
看見它們自己進行季節性的更新，
我短暫的存在時光僅是一生一死，
不朽只是在字典裡的措辭。

II. Life Perspectives

I see myself no different from leaves of a tree,
Experiencing cyclical flourishing and dying fate,
Except I am not as versatile as the tiny plants,
Seeing themselves go through seasonal rebirth,
My transient existence is once in a life time,
Immortality is only a definition in the dictionary.

578　鼠年的意識

我們不過是一群演員，
輕率的在台上或台下表演，
其間我們講究的穿戴去引人注目，
我們讀書與寫作來娛樂自己，
最後，我們都修飾簡單的離去。

我們所作所為全是付債，
對家庭、對傳統或對社會，
無形，無實體仍難以忍受，
在神志清醒或在不自覺之下，
它們像我們背著的行李醒或睡。

我們充分的覺得我們不是單獨，
在我們之內都有暗藏的力量。
我們帶著他們好像梳子或牙刷，
在青年的時期您依賴他們，
當您光頭和無牙之時你就完全忽略。

有良心或者是有責任感，
一個挽救臉面或挽救榮耀的象徵，
善惡或是文雅與殘暴，
我們對失敗的恐怖僅是懼怕的自己。

我們為過去的不足道而擔心，
記憶是領悟而沒有個體，
它能溫和我們的心胸也能分裂，
寫著作品是一種過程和發洩，
讓記憶從貯藏中外流，
然而對別人它是毫無意義的感受。

2008年2月7日 鼠年

578   **Rats' Year Mentality**

We are only a bunch of actors,
Performing indiscreetly on or off the stages,
In between, we dress nicely to impress others,
And we read and write to amuse ourselves,
In the end, we depart and dress simply.

What we do and say is paying debts,
To family, to tradition or to society,
Invisible , insubstantial and yet very heavy,
Conscious or unconscious matters little,
We bear them like baggage asleep or awake .

We are fully aware that we are not alone,
There is always a hidden force within us.
We carry them as if a comb or toothbrush,
In youth, we depend on them very greatly,
We ignore them when bald and toothless.

With conscience or sense of duty,
An emblem in saving face or saving glory,
Good or evil and gentle or ferocious,
The terror of failure is only the fear itself.

We dread worthlessness as part of our past,
The memory has no entity but awareness,
It warms our heart and yet tears it apart,
Writing it down is a process and an outlet,
To let remembrance flow out of reservoir,
It is meaningless to impress others.

Feb. 7, 2008 Year of Rat

585　客觀與主觀的現實

在覺醒和做夢的交點，
我們漂泊進出領悟和神志清楚。
在客觀與主觀的現實是枕頭，
其意念是軟和溫暖的床，
在接觸和氣味感覺的之外，
對誰我會贈送我的敬畏？

世界是真正的反常和變化莫測，
毫無真誠和意氣相投，
我們用花言巧語但缺乏感受，
我們取樂以無聊的幽默但並不快樂，
你不可能分辨他們銷售的好行為，
還是為他們自己贏利詐欺或蒙蔽，
荒涼的世界您不能信賴任何人，
也許我們應該負一部分責備。

越大的曝露您就越寒冷，
較小的寬度只影響小範圍，
最大的周界影響人類。
我們創造地球暖化和冰河時代，
我們要按的鈕是我們的意志，
我們的頭與大腦在我們的肩背，
用不用它完全靠我們自己的智慧。

忍耐的力量不是勝利或失敗，
它有排斥不幸和悲傷的力量，
和吸收誤解和外在的卑劣，
人的道德不是他們的財富而是品格，
聲望是來自他們的行動而不是他們所說，
為誰我才能寄託我的信仰及期待。

2008 年 3 月 10 日

585   **Objective and Subjective Reality**

At the focal point of awaking and dreaming,
We drift in and out of conscious and awareness.
The objective and the subjective reality is pillow,
And the sense of the soft and warm bed,
Beyond the feeling of touch and smell,
To whom do I bestow my attentiveness?

The world is truly erratic and unpredictable,
And devoid of sincerity and congeniality,
They speak colorful words but lack sensibility,
Laugh at the silly humor but short of happiness,
One can never tell whether they sale good deeds,
Or scams and deceptions for their own profit,
What a desolate world where you can trust no one,
Perhaps we are responsible for part of the blame.

The larger the exposure the cold you get,
Small width only influences the local scale,
Maximum perimeter affects the humanity.
We create globe warming and ice age,
The button we have to push is in our own will,
Our head is on our shoulder with cereal cortex,
Use it or not is entirely up to our intellect.

Power of endurance is not to win or to lose,
It has the force to repel misfortune and sadness,
And absorb blunders and external unfairness,
Morality of man is not their wealth but character,
Character is by their action not what they say.
And for whom do I place my trust and faith.

Mar 10, 2008

587　從我處於有利的論點

從我處於有利論點的今天，
我享受神聖自由的特權，
沒有阻礙及職責的義務，
沒有人不留情的在我背後，
監視我是否履行我該做的手藝。

我們由命運和機會而出生，
不由異想天開和熱誠的祈禱。
那裡有無數個培育的道路，
鑄造了我們今天是誰，
成功的結果只能來自汗水。

退休是一個新生活的開始，
當大多數要死的人都已死去，
即使我發現我被拋在後頭，
但我為新的遠景張開了我的眼睛，
而我對知識的渴望到達了頂點。

靈感來的時候不用聲明，
從誤解中誕生了瞭解，
才智是從博學中萌芽，
不忠常常是無生育的根源，
智慧來自成熟和年齡。

我看著在我視窗外面騷亂的世界，
我平安自足的欣賞音樂和詩篇，
即使我明天也許會死，
我今天仍是活潑的自我陶醉，
或許我有點悲觀但總是樂觀主義，
我不能改變我過去的發生，
而又憂慮的希望將來，
結局完全基於我命運的好壞。

2008 年 3 月 13 日

587   **From my Vantage Point**

From the vantage point of today,
I enjoy the sacred freedom of my liberty,
Without hinder and obligation of duty,
Or anyone relentlessly hanging behind my back,
Whether I keep my end of bargain for my trade.

We were born through destiny and chance,
Not by wishful thinking and hearty prayer.
There are infinitive paths in upbringing,
That molded us into who we are today,
The outcome can only be achieved by sweat.

Retirement was the beginning of a new life,
When most of the mortals have been died,
Even though I discovered I was left behind,
But I opened my eyes for the new prospect,
While my thirst of knowledge reached its apex.

Inspiration comes without declaration,
Understandings born from misunderstandings,
Intelligence sprouts from learned knowledge,
Infidelity frequently is the root of infertility,
Wisdom comes from maturation and age.

I see the world hurly-burly outside of my window,
I am peacefully content with music and poetry.
Even if I may die tomorrow,
I still would be lively myself today,
Pessimistic perhaps but optimistic always,
I could not alter what has happened in my past,
And apprehensively hopeful for the future,
The conclusion is entirely resting on my fate.

March 13, 2008

588　春分隨筆

我們歸因於我們不知道的事是邪惡，
但不認為我們心胸狹窄。
我們信任我們的信仰是神聖和公平，
而不知道我們自己的無知和偏見。

在白天的中午它不可能是午夜，
除非在一個全日蝕的地區。
如果夏至是在北回歸線上，
中午你將會沒有影子。

我們認為人在白天睡眠很不自然，
但忘記他們是在不同的時區，
日睡者也許有夜間的行業，
他們是否在醫院，在天文臺；
在後巷或在暗街上賣弄風情。

我們對批評很容易感到不安，
又為不合理的評斷悶悶不樂，
及對不經心的稱讚興高采烈，
即使風向輕微的變動，
我們心情從輕快轉變成悲哀。

好印象或壞記憶是瞬間性，
時間腐蝕我們鋒利的頭腦和輕快，
遲鈍我們的眼力和快速反應。
敵人善於利用我們的疏忽，
我們則缺乏我們智力的鍛煉。

我不是一位在修道院深淵的方丈，
亦不坐在臺上接受朝拜，
我寧可是一個平民而不是聖賢。
聖徒我不是，我也不是惡棍，
我既不渴望特權也不承受負擔。

2008年3月20日

588   **Gibberish on the Vernal Equinox**

We attribute things we don't know as evil,
Not thinking that we are narrow-minded.
We trust our belief to be sacred and just,
Not knowing our own ignorance and prejudice.

It cannot be midnight at the middle of the day,
Unless in the region of a total solar eclipse.
If you are on the Tropic of Cancer at noon,
It will be shadowless on the summer solstice.

We think people who sleeps in the day is weird,
But forget there are different time districts,
Day sleepers may have the night professions,
Whether they are in a hospital, in an observatory;
Walk in the back alley flirting on the dim streets.

We are disturbed easily by any criticism,
And deeply depressed by unfair judgment,
Yet excessively elated by casual praise,
With the slightest changes of the wind,
We swing our mood from gloom to gay.

Good impression or bad memory is transitory,
Time erodes our sharp mind and agility,
Dulls our eyesight and responsiveness
The enemy makes better use of our negligence,
We are lacking the exercise of our intelligence.

I am not an abbot in the abyss of an abbey,
Nor sit on the podium to receive homage,
I would rather be a common man than a sage.
Saint I am not, I am neither a villain,
I do not desire the privilege or the burden.

March 20, 2008

589 愚人節的漫筆

我很倔強但並不頑固,
我不告訴別人我多大年紀,
又希望他們認為
我比較年青。
年紀不是您多大,
而是您的感覺,
但不要期待鏡子會同意。
發熱感和關節酸痛都是現實。

我們知道痛是起自一定的年齡,
但是痛在任何年齡都是不自然,
當您在找您帽子的時候,
而不知道戴在您的頭上,
頭也許很強但敏感虛弱,
身體的活力壓倒,
知覺的不足。

我們變的更加肥胖和粗劣,
而且慢慢地滑入流沙的成年,
在落寞密林,
和無能的人間,
沒有人能伸出一隻援手。
當我們沉入深而迷惑不解,
我們開始拖延不可避免的局面。

我們大家都惦念模糊的過去,
又想從失掉信任的廢墟裡得到救濟。
而不是面對自然,
我們希望死亡會解決我們的問題。
死是很合理但是已經死了,
只有不知覺悟者仍然精神洋溢。

2008年4月1日

589   **April Fools' Essay**

I am headstrong but not mulish,
I don't wish to tell others how old I am,
And hope they will say,
I am not at my age.
Age isn't how old you are,
Only how old you feel,
But do not expect mirrors to agree,
Hotflashes and aching joints are real.

We know that pain is natural at a certain age,
But pain is unnatural at any age,
When you are searching for your hat,
And not knowing you wear it on your head,
Strong head perhaps but weak sensibility,
Bodily vigor overwhelms,
But lack awareness.

We are growing coarser and plumper,
And slowly slipping into the age of quicksand,
In the desolate jungle,
And world of feeble man,
No one is able to extend a helping hand.
As we sink into the fathomless fog,
We begin to defer our inevitable impasse.

Most of us hinge on a glimmer of the past,
And wish to salvage from the ruins of lost trust.
Rather than face the natural outcomes,
We hope death will resolve our problems.
The dead were rational but have died,
Only the less sensible are still alive.

April 1, 2008

591   徹查的經驗

我在一個大炸圓圈裡面伸展，
他們注射毒物染料進入我的靜脈，
空著肚子嘗著金屬味，
我只可以想像和恐懼為它的嗡嗡聲，
我的血液也許變成青色與骨肉透明，
那些無形的魔爪探查我的腸胃，
我的內臟毫無防禦有如玉米粥，
但他們不可能攫取我的知覺。

骨肉結實但易粉碎，
精神剛毅微妙但難以判決，
我們好像是一隻在蜘蛛網上無能的蒼蠅，
我們的血液是標本受注射槍豪飲，
我們的陰部讓他們撫弄和猛戳。
您可以剃、雕刻、殘害我的內臟，
我只會把我的心給我所愛的人。

噢! 多麼貧困的小屍體，
忍受無數的酷刑和苦難，
受到嚴重的飢餓與嚴寒，
我們認為我們的身體健康和強壯，
但它軟弱的如一隻小黃蜂，
一個在膝蓋上 抓痕或在手指割傷，
我們好像酒杯打碎在壁爐上。

一件小事鬧成一個大事件，
牙痛，緊急措施和電話，
冷漠診所不關心您的遭受，
但計較您的醫療保險，
我以為醫生是治療和屠夫是砍，
它只是好的價錢買頭等貨，
是否年齡使我冷嘲熱諷？
或者我是一名不寬容的患者？

591   **Scrutinized Experiences**

I am stretched inside a big doughnut,
They inject poison dye into my vein,
With an empty stomach and taste metallic,
I can only imagine and fear for its humming,
My blood may turn blue and flesh transparent,
Those invisible tentacles probe my abdomen,
My gut is defenseless and soft as mush,
But they cannot snap away my consciousness.

Muscles and bones are solid but fragile,
Mental fortitude is subtle but hard to measure,
We are helpless as if a fly on the spider web,
Our blood is specimens for syringes to swig,
Our private part is for them to fondle and jab.
You may shave, carve and mutilate my gut,
I will only give my heart to the one I love.

O! What an impoverished little carcass,
Endured for countless tortures and miseries,
Subjected to the bitter cold and severe hunger,
We thought our body strong and robust,
Yet it is feeble and frail as a tiny wasp,
One small scratch on knees or a cut on fingers,
We shatter as if a glass against the mantel.

A small freak incident flared into a big event,
Toothache, emergency schedule and phone calls,
The indifferent clinics mind not what you suffer,
But fret what your medical insurance can cover,
I thought physicians cure and butchers chop,
It is only the best price pays for the prime parts,
Has age made me skeptical and cynical?
Or am I an intolerant patient with no graciousness?

595　死亡和變形

死亡是終止或變形的別名，
一個新的領土隱喻的起點，
它是已知和未知之間分割，
是無形和非可通信的世界，
我們總覺得我們知道的是安全，
我們不能看見的可怕與不確定性。

無死亡的土地可能是混亂而不是太平，
除非老化與疾病是在等式的外面，
否則年輕人連續的出生，
老病和殘障壓制著風景。
人口過剩和飢荒把持地平線，
人類將被推入於不平衡。

我們把死亡等於是一種外流，
為平衡掃除老弱與厭惡，
一個沒有死亡的世界是無感情的世界。
老年醫學管理茂盛和葬禮服務處缺席，
惡棍是永遠不死而聖徒不見，
自殺事件僅存在於夢境。

法制系統興旺而醫學休眠，
明智者增長更明智貪婪者變得更貪心，
棺材製作人和壽保險而被消除，
戰爭和屠殺僅存在電子遊戲，
死亡與瘟疫僅是想像，
伊甸園的現實不是幻覺。

誰能想生命有更加愉快的境界？
沒有死亡的忘我境界填滿自然痛苦，
即使傻子也不一定那麼愚蠢的相信，
或去夢想許多人已做過的夢。
我會讓樂園給那些希望尋找的人，
接受我愚蠢家族天然的命運。

2008年5月1日

595 **Death and Transfiguration**

Death is an alias for ending or transfiguration,
The metaphorical beginning of a new realm,
It is a partition between known and unknown,
A world of invisibility and non-communication,
We always feel secure with what we know,
Fearful of uncertainty with things we cannot see.

Deathless land is likely in chaos not harmony,
Unless aging and illness is out of the equation,
Or else the young will be born continuously,
The old and sick overwhelm the landscape.
Overpopulation and famine will dominate horizon,
And humanity will be thrust into imbalance.

We equate death to a kindly outflow,
To get rid of old and abomination for equilibrium,
A world without death is unemotional world,
Geriatric cares flourish and funeral home absent,
Villains are immortal and Saints are missing,
The incident of suicide exists only in an illusion.

Legal systems thrive and medicine lies dormant,
Wise grows wiser and greedy becomes greedier,
Coffin makers and life insurance eliminated,
War and killings exist only in an electronic game,
Death and plague are merely in the imagination,
The reality of Garden of Eden is no longer fantasy.

Who can envision life in a happier state?
An ecstasy filled with natural agonies,
Even fools are not thick enough to believe,
Or dream the dreams that many have dreamt.
I will let paradise for those who wish to seek,
And accept my natural fate as the foolish ilk.

May 1, 2008

548　心神不定

十月 - 彩色的楓葉,
我觀看秋天的樹林,
注視下降的落葉,
我把它們裝入袋子中,
但明天還會再重復,
只有秋季獲勝。

我在院子裡東奔西走,
去察看我的菜園,
及季節結束的狼狽,

我用雜草去為它們保溫,
用落葉去隱匿它們,
試圖去蒙蔽行竊的野鹿,
最終野鹿仍然是成功。

我搬移木柴劈開樹木,
來減輕我僵硬的筋骨,
和靜坐在樹根上,
去聽落葉打擊著落葉,
螞蟻在樹葉下的忙碌。

當我再劈幾根木柴,
去打破一切的沈悶,
一整天的結尾, 筋疲力盡,
我發現我自己仍是心神不定。

548   **Restless**

Colorful foliage - October,
I observe autumn trees,
And watch the falling leaves,
I rake them and bag them,
But leaves will fall tomorrow again,
Only the autumn season wins.

I walk around in my yard,
To see my vegetable garden,
And their season ending predicament,

Using mulch I keep them warm,
And hide them with leaves,
Attempting to deceive the stealing deer;
In the end, the deer succeed.

I move logs and split wood,
To ease my stiffing bones,
And sit on the tree stump silently,
To hear falling leafs hitting leafs,
With ants busy underneath.

As I split a few more logs again,
To break the silence,
By end of the day, exhausted,
I found myself still restless.

598　無形的個體

睡覺是在生命中必然的一部分，
如我們吃東西是同樣的強制，
食物是為了腸胃飢餓的欲望，
而夢想卻是滿足精神的乾枯，
白日夢很激動人心但很危險，
過分放縱也許會導致不幸。

沒有什麼比夢更無從捉摸，
一個在它們自己設計和顯示的世界，
深不可測，地點和時間難定，
您既不能接觸和品嘗味道，
它們在進展中五顏六色及生動，
一旦行動停止卻是雨消雲散，
所留下的僅是睡眠的困乏。

我是一個不會夢想的人但富於睡眠，
過著簡單的生活既無花招又無彩飾，
我不祈求奇蹟也不打賭非可能性，
世界並不問我的觀點我亦不提供，
如果夢想不能提供激發或安心，
即使幻夢也不值得嚮往，
引喻然後就失掉它的刺激和線索。

當您設法去忘記令人不快的事件，
您的頭腦將強調他們更加卓越，
為了您不去想一件事，
您將必須把你的頭腦超載，
一個混濁的知覺是無辜的意識，
負擔的精神對恐嚇比較不甚危害。

老化在生命中有一點好處，
我們沒有多少愚蠢的幻覺與固執，
但經常懷有記憶的幻影，
未來是如此的不定與不明，
喜歡的記憶如糖漿一樣的甜蜜，
引喻就不能完全的避免。

2008 年 5 月 20 日

Amorphous Entity

Sleep is an essential component of life,
Same as the obligatory requirement of eat,
Food is for desire of the hungry stomach,
Dream in sleep satisfies brain's thirsty.
Dream in day is inspirational but dangerous,
Over-indulgence may lead to tragedy.

Nothing is more elusive than an illusion
A world in its own design and manifestation,
Fathomless, indefinable in time and space,
You can neither have the feeling of touch nor taste,
They are vivid and colorful while in progress,
But vanish into thin air once the action ceases,
What's lingering is the destitute of sleep.

I am a man poor in dreams but rich in sleep,
Living in a simple life without hype and pageantry,
I do not ask for miracle nor bet for impossibility,
The world ask me no opinion nor I offer any,
If dreams do not offer uplifting or relief,
Even dreams are not worthwhile to dream,
An allusion then loses its zest and hint.

When you try to forget an unhappy event,
Your mind will emphasize its eminence,
In order for you of not thinking one thing,
You will have to overload your brain,
A cloudy sense is an innocent mentality,
The burdened mind is less perilous to menace.

Growing old has one advantage in life,
We may have little foolish illusion and tenacity,
But often cherish in the apparition of memories,
Future is mucky at best and uncertain,
Fond remembrance is as sweet as molasses,
We are not totally immune from the allusion.

May 20, 2008

600　真理與正確

我們都很貪婪的有如照像機鏡頭，
沒有允許奪取他人的影像，
不管它是壞的時光或好的片刻，
但它卻代表最高的正直與真相，
我們不可能每分鐘多有適當的行動。
缺點不是急速拍攝的透鏡，
而是物體本身製造的欺騙。

日月蝕的創作是巧合，
地球內部的不穩引起地震，
閏年的設立是由於人的觀念，
龍捲風和旋風來自於大自然，
洪水與乾旱由雨量而產生，
那些不是眾神的錯誤或處罰，
人的愚昧不完全是沒有責任。

光亮對人民有它偏重的公正，
而光只照明半邊忽略其他，
黑暗以相等的威嚇吞沒一切。
我們修築隱藏處所擋風和避難，
水在它的管轄之下侵略所有裂縫。
我們可以貯藏它們用來灌溉和發電，
你不可能把光存在瓶子裡來照明。

地球的移動調控我們的活動，
水向下流是起自重力，
由於壓力的梯度吹風使其平衡，
花開是迎接春天的來臨，
冷熱的氣候是季節的變換。
那些不是反常或是不完全，
真正的缺陷是我們缺乏認識。

2008 年 5 月 27 日

600   Truth and Validity

We are all greedy like a camera lens,
Snatching others' images without permit,
Whether it is a good moment or bad break,
It presents the highest truth and integrity,
We cannot act appropriately every minute.
The fault is not the lens that does its snapping,
It is the object itself fabricating the deception.

The creation of eclipses was by coincidence,
Earthquakes caused by the shaky earth interiors,
Leap years were established by concept of man,
Tornados and cyclones made by fury of nature,
Flood and drought created by the amount of rain,
Those were not god's errors or punishments,
Man's ignorance was not totally without blame.

Brightness has a lopsided fairness to its subjects,
While light enlightens one half ignore the rest,
Darkness devours everything with equal menace.
We built shelter to shear off wind and take refuge,
Water invades every bit of crack in its dominion.
We stash them away for irrigation and electricity,
You can never store light in a bottle for illumination.

The movements of earth regulate our activities,
Water flows downhill because of gravity,
Wind blows to equalize gradients of pressure,
Flowers blossom in greeting the coming of spring,
And hot and cold climate is the changing of seasons.
Those are not abnormal or imperfection,
The real flaw is we lack understandings.

May 27, 2008

602　道德的尺度

在黑暗沈靜的深夜，
我們搜尋失去的靈魂。
在喧嚷吵鬧的日光，
人格的攻擊沒有界限，
我們消耗神聖的精髓好像劣貨。

頻率的多少來建立音調，
單獨音波起伏難能共鳴，
快的節拍與高能相關，
我們使用紅色象徵著危險，
但藍光與紫外線有殺害生命的能力。

孤零零的音符不製造音樂，
多節奏乃能創造音調及歌曲，
雜亂聲響引起噪音與騷動，
韻詩不能在混亂的場合上演，
橫蠻的暴民易於導致混亂。

道德價值是與時間和空間相對，
我們如嬰兒的裸露來到這個世界，
密林的部落習慣的暴露他們的肌肉，
裸體在私下是很自然與美觀，
在公共場所暴露是粗鄙與不合時宜。

沒有看見的犯罪也許會逃脫司法，
共謀常會發生在二者之間，
在眾人之前發生的罪行不可能逃避處罰，
自我懲罰是起自以內在的良心，
道德是由目擊者的多少來判定。

2008年6月5日

602   **Scale of Morality**

In silence of the dark night,
We are searching for the lost soul.
In the boisterously bright daylight,
Character assassination has no boundary,
We spend our divine core as if trash.

Number of frequency makes pitch of sound,
A pulsation of single wave gives no resonance,
Faster the beats correlate with higher energy,
We use red color to symbolize danger,
The farmful rays are blue and ultraviolet.

A solitary note does not make music,
Multiple rhythms create songs and melodies,
Disorderly sounds generate clatter and noise,
Rhymes do not perform in the crowd of chaos,
The unruly mob is likely to cause turmoil.

Moral value is relative in time and space,
We were naked as an infant came into this world,
Jungle tribes habitually exposing their flesh,
Nude in private is beauty and nature,
Bare all in public is indecent and inappropriate.

Felony may escape justice without bystanders,
Conspiracy could exist between two friends,
Crime occurring in crowd can't evade punishment,
Self-incrimination is conscience arises within,
Morality is measured by number of witnesses.

June 5, 2008

603　幻覺與現實

我們所看見和聽見都是幻覺，
有意或無意為我們創立，
我們所察覺也許是實際或錯誤，
他們只是短暫的存在而無觸覺。
我所盼望的從未實現，
我沒有期待的經常逼迫我容忍。
或許這是正常性的定義，
只有您的自我意識才是現實。

生活是在無休止奮鬥的一個過程，
我們所作所為遭受到批評或認同，
我們所說經常引起爭執或辯論。
準則使我們服從原理與規則，
家庭和學校迫使我們遵守指示，
我們聽他們評斷與裁決，
我們的思想可能非法的被侵佔。

我們持續不斷的等待上蒼的救助，
而且對上天與世間要求解除。
凡人與不朽之間的距離浩大，
我們所有的禱告和啼哭消失到虛無。
你能看見遍地的淚花，
神聖從不和睦與同情，
他們選擇誰而來覺得他們的可憐？

如果我不哭是因為我已經哭夠了，
我不去乞求因為沒人給予任何關心，
如果您認為事事美好它將會成真。
健康、美麗、財富和勢力是相對，
世事沒有測量的絕對標準，
我們都有情感和感傷的偏心，
並且以我們當時的感覺去評定。

603   Illusion versus Reality

What we see and hear are all illusions,
Creating for us with or without intent,
What we perceive may be real or false,
Exist only momentarily without feel.
What I had hoped for never materialized,
What I didn't expect often was thrust upon me.
Perhaps this is the definition of normality,
Only your self-awareness is the reality.

Life is a process in the never-ending struggle,
What we do to subject criticism or approval,
What we say often causing debate or controversy.
Norms make us to obey rules and principles,
Family and school force us to follow instructions,
We listen to them for verdict and judgment,
Our thought could be invaded by exploitation.

We waited incessantly for the divine deliverance,
And turn to heaven and earth for relief.
The space between mortal and immortal is vast,
All of our prayers and cries lost in the void.
There are tears everywhere you can see,
The divinity never in tune with such sympathy,
Whom do they select to feel their pities?

If I do not cry because I have cried enough,
I do not beg and no one has paid any attention.
If you think that thing is beautiful then it will be,
Beauty, health, power and wealth are relative,
There are no absolute standards to gauge.
We are all emotional and sentimental with bias,
And judge things at the moment how we feel.

604 獨立性

當我們在世界的高峰，
我們從未感覺在深淵底部的疼痛。
有些人因為他們的行為而被推下山，
其他的由於輪子的轉動而被拋開。
我由我的自願而離棄動亂的世界，
只想被人遺忘去找一點平靜。
無所需求才是最後的安寧。

我不是領導人和指導其他帶領者，
也不是一個盲目的追隨者，
主體和客體之間的區別是圖像，
主觀和客觀不同的是目的，
疑義養殖憂慮和憂慮釀造秘訣，
失望激發動機與機巧，
缺乏欲望提供悠閒與自由。

惡劣行為是來自邪惡的頭腦，
黑色染料只能染白色灰白和黑暗，
溫厚的品格不僅是來自偽善，
而且也來自環境和教養，
敏感性是覺悟的根源，
施惠者或受惠者的區別僅是知覺性，
從虛構中分出真理是由於證據。

當我們的世界在收縮與崩潰，
在末端有個聚合點，
那裡一切變得不能分離而且視覺泥濘，
個別性將被隱蔽得糊塗不清，
在這些淩亂的情況下生存，
我們需要為自己退後一步建立空間，
哲學家不是在混亂無知中誕生。

2008 年 6 月 20 日夏至

604 Individuality

When we are on the top of the world,
We never feel the pain at the bottom of the abyss.
Some were pushed off because of their behaviors,
Other just fell off due to the turning of wheels.
I left the world of turmoil by my own free will,
Longing to be left alone and find some peace,
The ultimate of tranquility is absence of need.

I was neither a leader, who led the leaders,
Nor a follower who followed blindly,
Subject and object differ by image we see,
Subjective and objective is different in the aim,
Doubt breeds anxiety and anxiety brews secrecy,
Desperation ferments motivation and ingenuity,
The lack of desire provides a leisure and liberty.

Malicious conduct is from evil mind,
Black dye will only dye white to grey or black,
Good character is not only by self-righteous,
But also by up-bringing and environment,
Sensitivity is the root of awareness,
Giver or taker's difference is only consciousness,
Truth separating from fiction is by evidence.

As our world shrinks and collapses,
There is a converging point at the end,
Where things are inseparable and view is muddy,
Individuality will be smothered to become cloudy,
To exist in all these cluttered circumstances,
We need to step-back making space for identity,
Philosopher is not made from muddled ignorant.

June 20, 2008 Summer Solstice

605　在薄霧中漫遊

一批黃色的小花，
突出一片白色三葉草，
混合著數片紅葉，
又被原野的青草皮而淹沒。
太陽以相等的強度養育它們，
在生命中的適應性是生存鑰匙，
自然選擇確定它們的超越。

露水閃耀著在蜘蛛網上，
生命的掙扎會打破平靜，
粗心大意漫遊者可能會遭殃，
證據顯示那裡沒有勝敗。
在這不斷變化的情況和場面，
或許這是一場好的結尾。

曠野浩大而道路繁多，
它們總是在那裡讓您採納，
正確或錯誤僅是旅客的過失。
有些路也許很吵鬧、彎曲與漫長，
不熟悉 的捷徑也許是很冒險，
人類本性的精華是尋找未知，
這表示人與野獸之間的不同。

我們從草原看見的好像是面鏡子，
沒有官能的感受所構成的二維，
當我們轉頭之間所有圖像消失，
它們正如薄霧一樣的透明，
看見或看不見與它的真實性毫不相關，
他們都像故事中所說一樣的虛構。

2008 年 7 月 11 日

605   **Wandering in the Mist**

A small batch of tiny yellow flowers,
Protruding out from a patch of white clovers,
Mixing with a few blades of red leaves,
And overwhelmed by acres of green turf,
Sun nourishes them with equal intensity,
Adaptability of survival in life is the key;
Natural selection determines their superiority.

The morning air is cool and fresh,
Dew drops sparkle on a spider's web,
Life struggles would shatter the serenity,
Careless wanderers will likely be the casualty,
Evidence suggests there is no victim or champion.
In the ever-changing circumstance and scenery,
Perhaps this is one occasion for a good ending.

The field is vast and roads are many,
They are always there for you to take,
Right or wrong is only a traveler's mistake.
Some roads may be rowdy, curvy and long,
Short cut of the unfamiliar path may be risky,
The essence of human nature is to seek the unknown,
This marks the differences between man and beast.

What we see in a meadow as if in the mirror,
A two dimensional construct without sensual feel,
As our head turns and all images disappear,
They are just as transparent as the thin mist,
Seeing it or not is irrelevant to its authenticity,
They are all like fabrication once told in a story.

July 11, 2008

606   森林裡的字詞

圖書館是書和樹林的彙集,
他們令人尊敬與敬畏,
沈默、神奇、明智和莊嚴,
我們看見在架子上五顏六色的封面,
而不是樹在森林裡被犧牲的手腿。

我們看不見森林裡有書或圖書館裡有樹,
也不關心 他們是親屬或兄弟姊妹。
愚昧的知覺是虛弱的鏈接,
圖書館只是給蠢才去閱讀,
那些靈巧的人在街去學習。

以往字詞雕刻在石頭和介殼上,
不久之前我們完全使用紙張,
恐龍的遺骸被做成硬盤替換了樹,
從每頁數字到兆百萬位元記憶,
好像種子一代傳一代的培養洞察力。

我們看不見字的多種意義,
只使用最流行的片語,
一個字的用語太多成語又太老套,
我們常常未能理解的使用它們,
非正確的字義會傷害到你的尊嚴。

「一帆風順」是行程「一路平安」的口語,
但套住是拴住,而詭計是圈套,
向碼頭拋繩索沒有套上是一種難看,
在路上搭便車是旅行是一種方案,
或許我太愚蠢的很想埋怨。

2008 年 7 月 20 日

606   **Words in Forest**

Library is the collection of books and trees,
They are awesome in scope and with respects,
Silent, mysterious, wise and majestic,
We see them on shelves with colorful covers,
Not trees in forest sacrificing their arms and legs.

We rarely see books in forest or trees in the library,
And hardly care they are cousins or relatives,
Ignorant attentiveness is only the weak link.
Library is only for idiots, who want to read,
Those smart ones only learn from streets.

Words were carved on stones and shells,
Not so long ago we exclusively use paper,
Dinosaurs' remains made into disks replace trees,
From a few words per page to terabytes memories,
Nurturing insights generation to generation as if seeds.

We don't see all multiple definitions of words,
Only use their popular and common descriptions,
The word is too wordy and an idiom is too axiomatic,
We often use them casually without comprehension;
Inappropriate wordings are harmful to your esteem.

"Bon Voyage" is "Without a Hitch" for a trip,
But a hitch is a catch and the catch is snatch,
To cast a line to a pier without hitch is a glitch,
To fetch a ride on highway is hitchhike,
Perhaps I am too foolish with the itch to bitch.

July 20, 2008

607　種子的分類

小的如針尖大的如松果或椰子，
輕的像羽毛，亮的如銀珠又滑的像鰻魚，
他們在天空飛又牢牢的拴住您的衣襟，
您用網捉住他們和從海裡撈，
在花園裡發芽和在田野裡播種，
收穫為食物和肉一起烹煮。
為鳥、草坪、婚禮或椅墊，
您用大袋子或小包裹的去買賣。

他們是堅果、核桃和愛心，
細菌、毒菌和病毒的起源，
它們有些甚難培養，
其他的又傾覆您的草地和景觀，
多數人大畢支付去驅除和毀壞它們，
其他大事花費養育它們去開花，
又有少數人去做買賣賺得成千上萬元。

您壓榨它們做油、花生醬或漿糊，
作為調味香料和裝飾他們在蛋糕，
把它們磨成粉或氣化它們成液體，
煮沸它們做清湯、濃湯或稀飯，
發芽啟發智慧和靈感，
或隱藏仇恨的想法和惡行，
和您夢想成名但從未成功。

我們來自它，離開時又把它埋沒，
我們每次生一個，兩個但很少是三胞胎，
有四個腿的牲畜卻生許多動物，
魚和鳥龜在河海位置下成千上萬卵，
人工受精製造多重嬰兒來競爭。
果子核由它們的肉體來包裹，
哺乳動物由子宮和子宮體來庇護，
昆蟲把它們用絲綢包在繭內。

噢！多美妙，神奇的種子。

2008年7月22日

607 Taxonomy of Seeds

Tiny as a pin tip and huge as coconut or pine cone,
Light as feather, slippery as eel and shiny as bead,
They fly in the air and fasten on to your socks or sleeves,
You catch them with a net and fish them from sea,
Sprout them in garden and sow them in field,
And harvest for food and cook them with meat.
For birds, for lawn, for weddings or for seat,
You buy them in large bags or in small packages.

They are nuts, walnut and heart of love,
The origin of germs, bacteria and virus,
Some of them are difficult to cultivate,
Others overwhelm your yard and landscapes,
Most pay a bundle to get rid of and to mutilate them,
Others spend amply to nourish them into flowering,
And a few make earn millions just to deal with it.

You press them to make oil, peanut butter or paste,
Using them as seasoning and decorating them on a cake,
Grinding them into flour or pulverizing them into liquid,
Boiling them to make broth, soup or porridges,
Springing thought of wisdom, fruit of an inspiration
Or harboring ideas of hatred and evil,
And dream successes you never succeed.

We came from it and bury it when we leave,
We give birth one at a time, or two and rarely triplet,
Four legged animals produce many puppies,
Fishes and turtles lay millions of eggs in rivers or seas,
Intro-fertilization makes multiple babies to compete.
Fruits pits wrapped around by their flesh,
Mammals shelter embryo by wombs and uterus,
Insects cocoon themselves in a pouch with silk.

Oh! What a wonderful, miraculous seed.

July 22, 2008

608 在幻覺裡的凹痕

我們生命資料是公開紀錄，
血壓、膽固醇、脫氧核糖核酸或心電圖，
但我們掩藏我們的體重和年齡。
大肆花費來整形我們的外表，
但我們毫無改造內在的真誠與賢良，

人們雅致的穿戴掩蓋他們的皮膚，
但忽略他們精神溫暖和端莊。
我們付去高價拍攝名人的臉面，
但不會對無家可歸者掃視一眼，
閉上眼睛不會減少社會弊病。

我們孵出一幫劣貨來破壞我們的聲望，
競選僅是把陳腐不中用的傢夥扔掉，
而招致新的面目也是鬼一樣的可憐。
投票者把他們的眼睛罩上顏色，
用性別與膚色來歪曲他們的意見，

您對上帝的祈禱是最神聖的深思，
而不是在「哭牆」留下便條。
如果崇拜成為競選活動的一部分，
我們不妨在聖誕節前寫信給聖誕老人。

我們急切的計數我們擁有小包裹，
但當我們有成千上萬的時候只是估計。
貧窮的人憂慮晚餐有什麼可吃，
富裕的煩惱要如何減肥。

我們都會大膽的推銷我們的見解，
趕緊的進行對友誼危害的裁決，
缺乏專心是唯一微弱的鏈接。
我們經常鎖前門擋君子，
但為便利和壞蛋半開後門。

2008 年 7 月 28 日

608   **Dents in Illusion**

Our vital statistics are public record,
Blood pressure, cholesterol, EKG or DNA,
But we hide our superficial weight and age.
We spend handsomely to reshape our looks
But not our virtues for sincerity and truthfulness,

People dress elegantly to cover their skins,
But neglect warmth and decency in their spirit.
We pay dearly to snap the faces of celebrities,
But would not cast a glance at the homeless,
Close your eyes will not diminish the social ills,

We hatch a bunch of bums to ruin our prestige,
The election is only by throwing old bums out,
And bringing in the new face is just as ghastly.
Voters put color shades in front their eyes,
Biasing their views on gender and skin-color.

It is the most sacred meditation you pray to God,
Not leaving a written note at the Wailing Wall.
If worship is becoming part of a stumping,
We might as well write to Santa before Christmas.

We anxiously count small numbers we own,
But only estimate them when we have millions.
Poor people worry what to eat for next meal,
Wealthy ones agonize how to rid of obesity.

We are all bold to thrust our personal opinion,
Rushing to pass judgment on friends is hazardous,
The lack of attentiveness is the only weak link.
We often lock the front door to bar gentlemen,
But jar back door for villains and conveniences .

July 28, 2008

609　安地斯山的拾零

在那些遙遠的安地斯山脈，
乾燥無際的沙漠及稀疏的居民，
那是天文學家修造他們天文臺的場所，
一條彎曲的道路沿著山谷及山坡，
汽車飛奔、灰塵飛騰、陰影跟蹤。
除了幾個仙人掌山上全無草木。
片片的白雲點綴著藍天，
微風軟軟地的撫弄傾斜神鷹飛舞。

在群山之中風景蕭條，
直到日光消散黑暗低沉，
西方天空充滿紅色面紗。
在晚上金黃煥發退色之後，
無月的夜空炫耀的星光，
在平靜和安寧的山頂上，
稀薄的大氣使您感覺飄飄如仙，
終究這是我去天堂最接近的地點。

黑暗的晚上莊嚴，安靜和雄偉，
機械的聲音打破夜空的沈默。
漫長的無眠夜最後接近尾聲，
黑暗帷幕疊起而讓了步，
安地斯山峰被早晨微明而吞沒。
夜間的活動停止返回休息，
塵世生活恢復他們的每日花招。

當山下的世界催促與奔忙，
無裂縫的日程表，繁瑣與忙碌，
在山上所有的日眠者正在夢鄉。
在極短的時間與極少數夜晚，
他們都希望達到最大成效。
在此被隔絕和荒涼的山頂，
行動及思想的都傾向於視覺，
安地斯山，神秘的探測都是地方化。

609   **Tidbits of Andes**

On those remote mountains of Andes,
Sparse inhabitant miles around and dry desert,
That's where astronomers built their observatories,
A winding road curves along the valleys and hills,
Cars dash, dusts soar and shadows follow.
The mountains are grassless except a few cacti.
Patches of white clouds spot the blue sky,
Wind softly caresses the slopes where condors fly.

The landscapes among themselves are dull,
Not until the end of sunsets and darkness falls,
Western horizon fills with reddish color veils.
After the fading of evening golden glow,
Moonless night starlight dazzles,
On the peaceful and tranquil mountain top,
Thinner atmosphere rousing you a feeling of high,
After all, this is the closest I will ever get to heaven.

The dark evening is majestic, grand and quiet,
The sounds of machinery break the silent night.
The long sleepless night finally draws to a close,
Curtain of darkness has folded up and withdrawn,
Crests of Andes engulfed with the morning twilight,
Nocturnal activities cease and return to rest,
Earthly lives resume their daily habit.

While the world hustles and bustles below,
The seamless schedule is hectic and tedious,
All the day-sleepers are in dream land.
In the minimum interval of handful nights,
They all wish to achieve the maximum heights.
On top of this isolated and desolate mountain,
Action and mindset are restricted to visual sight,
Exploration to the mystic of the Andes is localized.

這離人類很遠的地方沒有社交活動，
觀看壯觀的日落和兔狐狩獵，
變得是我們在晚餐後難免的娛樂。
看見強大兀鷹的飛行是高潮，
但不要等到它們來得太進而感到不安，
當振動的羽毛嘶嘶聲飛過幾尺之外，
巨型翼展，敬畏的爪和不祥的眼睛，
您但願不是它們的晚餐。

1989 年 8 月 在托羅羅山，智利

兔狐: 南美挖洞大草原的嚙齒目動物，以兔頭及狐尾為特色，與黃鼠系關連。

兀鷹： 安地斯山大兀鷹，全身黑色羽毛和柔軟的頸毛，翼幅大約 12 英尺，現在幾乎絕種。

後記

每年降雨量少於半寸和在海拔約 11,000 英尺，北智利，位於在安地斯山西部邊緣，是世界其中一個最佳為光學天文觀測的站點。實際上，在智利北拉色琳納鎮 50 英哩內，有三個主要觀測天文臺，包括美國在南美托羅羅山國家天文臺，歐洲在拉夕亞南美聯盟天文臺和卡內基和加拿大在拉斯坎帕拉斯山天文臺。每晚約有三百位天文學家和電子技術支持人員整夜工作，使用世界最大和最先進的望遠鏡。拉色琳納鎮不僅以它的天文臺為名，而且也為它的海灘、美女和酒出名。

There are little social events this far from humanity,
Watching the spectacular sunset and viscachas[1] hunt,
Turn to our faithful after dinner entertainment.
To see the flight of the mighty condor[2] is a highlight,
But, not until it is become too close for comfort,
With the vibrating feather whooshing a few feet away,
Giant wing span, awesome claws and ominous eyes,
You wish you are not his dinner for the night.

Aug. 1989 on Cerro Tololo, Chile

[1] Viscacha: Burrowing rodents of the South American
Pampas, with rabbit head and fox tall, related to the Chinchilla's family.

[2] Condor: Large vulture of the Andes, black plumage, and a ruff of downy white feathers, and wingspread to 12 feet. It is now nearly extinct.

Epilog

With less than half-inch of rainfall per year and at an elevation more than 11,000 feet, Northern Chile, situated at the western rims of Andes, is one of the best sites for the Optical Astronomical Observations. Within 50 miles of La Serina, Chile, there are three major observatories, including the Inter-American Observatory of USA at Cerro Tololo, European Southern Observatory at La Silla and Carnage and Canadian Observatory at Las Campanas. More than three hundreds astronomers, supporting technicians and personnel work there, using the world some largest telescopes and most advanced electronics. The City of La Serina is not only famous for its observatories, but also for its beaches, beautiful women and wines.

768　一種蕭條的感受

我是個卑劣的說明者和畫家，
在幻想中描述一個扁平的世界，
見解都是黑或是白，
喜歡用惡劣字來寫作，
樹木既無葉子又無陰影，
這僅是一個陰雨的秋天，
世界不是那麼蕭條與單調。

我看見太陽從邊緣彈出和沉入，
日夜並不混合，
鳥在地上走而不是空中飛，
陸地沒有山峰或山谷，
回音只是想像中的錯覺。
我所看見的是短暫的世界，
我才是一個缺少夢想及想像白癡。

多數的幻夢都是不愉快，
夢想有最終的力量，
來與去毫無妨礙，
干擾我們的睡眠，
無夢的睡眠就像無穿梭紡織機，
像沒有沙丘的大沙漠，
在平坦沙漠中的海市蜃樓仍是夢。

睡著了之後我們無法控制，
夢指使私人和公眾的片刻，
保守秘密是當你活著或醒著的時候，
不是你在手術台與停屍間，
在臨終的床上沒有優雅，
無知覺的恥辱是一種無深淺感觸，
死了之後就無屈辱。

我們不是為死亡祈禱是為生存，
所有祈禱都是自私的定向，
為寬恕與願望討價還價，

768   A Sense of Flatness

I am a poor illustrator and artist,
Depicting a flat world in my mind,
Thinking in black and white,
Trees have neither leaves nor shadows,
Grasses wrinkled and flowers faded.
It is only a rainy autumn day,
The world is not so bleak and flat.

I see sun pops out and sinks into edges,
Day does not mix with night,
Birds walk not fly,
Mountains or valleys are absent,
Echo is only in the imagination,
I see the world in transience,
I am the idiot lacking dream and imagination.

Dreams are generally unpleasant,
It has the ultimate power,
And comes and goes without hinder,
Interfering with our sleep,
Yet dreamless sleep is shuttle-less loom,
Similar to a desert without sand dunes,
Mirage in a flat desert is still a delusion.

We have no control once falling asleep,
It manifests private and public moments,
Privacy is when you are alive or awake,
Not on a gurney or in a morgue,
There is no grace in the dying bed,
Unconscious mortification is a flat sensation,
And there is no humiliation after death.

We don't pray for death only survival,
All prayers have selfish goals,
Bargaining for desire and forgiveness,

祈禱像是利用空氣與空間，
它們無疑問又無限制，
直到我們陷入羅網或窒息之後，
我們才會懇求它的稀罕。

不要責怪思想創建熱望，
我們的肌體執行我們的行為，
當肉體粉碎與腐朽，
思想和願望也與身體消失不見，
一切都這消散去空間，
遺留的只有個小甕或是一堆泥土。

我不知道我死後會看見什麼，
是否是完全黑暗或明亮，
或者是東倒西歪的走或滑行。
我從不是奸賊也不是聖賢，
除了智慧與知識並不偷拿，
愛我自己從沒有殺過任何人，
也許 - 我不會完全看見黑暗

Prayer is like utilizing air and space,
They are there unlimited without query.
We only beg for them in scarcity,
When we are suffocating or entrapped.

We blame mind for creates craving,
It is our body performing our action,
When flesh crumbles and decays,
Mind and desire vanish with the body,
Everything dissipates into space,
Remaining is a tiny urn or a pile of soil.

I don't know what I will see after I die,
Whether it is perpetually dark or bright,
Or I stumble along or glide.
I have never been a villain or a saint,
Stole nothing but wisdom and knowledge,
Love myself and never killed anyone,
Perhaps - I will not see total darkness.

611 人類還有希望

在運動場裡有運動員和觀眾，
競爭者競爭教練們教練，
優勝者在壯觀波浪的前鋒，
歡樂，慶祝及享受榮耀，
失敗者消失於人群痛擊他們的失敗，
經理，教練和治療師留後，
計劃與準備下一節時間。

中國為奧林匹克比賽花費了億萬元，
展出使人目炫開幕式和輝煌的煙火，
我們看見鼓手人及在體育場內的瀑布，
一個在夜空裡行走的腳印，
我們看見一個幸運從地震生存的小男孩。
而不是生命的滅亡和可怕破壞，
我們聽見小女孩的歌聲與一張捏造的臉，
但忽略了數以萬計受害者的哀啼。

俄國人不讓中國人有全部的榮耀，
以侵略佐治亞國創造他們自己的煙花，
而他們的領導在體育場內戴上假的笑臉。
數百個國家在爭奪少數幾枚金牌，
成千上萬觀眾在世界每個角落，
誰注意到在戰爭中婦女和小孩的啜泣？
只有坦克和炸彈征服最後的戰地。

我應該感到驕傲或是恥辱身為中國人？
或大聲的尖叫去歡呼或抗議？
我太遙遠又無作為的不能有所影響，
以及那些在胡同廢墟裡老而皺紋的臉，
世界僅僅看見在螢幕上的精采，
只有誰能付得起高價入場簽，
才有幾秒鐘歡呼與興高采烈。

體育比賽與戰爭沒有不同，
真正的英雄在跑道上飛奔和在泥中爬，
在絕望中跌倒或被路旁炸彈炸，

611   **Hope in Humanity**

There are athletes and audiences in the arena,
Competitors compete and coaches coach,
Winners ride in the front of the wave in pageantry,
Festivities, celebrations, and enjoy glories,
Losers fade into the crowds and lick their defeats,
Managers, trainers and therapists stay behind,
Plan and prepare for the next period.

China spent billions for the Olympic Games,
Put up the pyrotechnical opening ceremony,
We see drummers and waterfalls in the stadium,
Night sky air foot-prints from a man walking,
We see a lucky boy survived from the earthquake.
Not the horrendous devastations and destructions,
We hear the voice of a little girl with a fabricated face,
But ignore tens and thousands' cries of victims.

Russians would not let the Chinese have all the glory,
By invading Georgia to create their own fireworks,
Yet their leaders in the stadium put up a false smile.
Hundreds nations competing for the few gold medals,
Millions of viewers in every corner of the world,
Who noticed women and children's weeps?
Only tanks and bombs conquer the battle field.

Should I be proud or mortified being a Chinese?
Or scream at the top of my lungs in protests?
I am too remote and insignificant to be of consequence,
Nor those old wrinkled faces in the ruins of Hutongs*,
The world sees merely what's splendid on screens,
Only who can pay the hefty price for an admission,
Get a few seconds of hoopla in cheering.

Sport events are no different from wars,
The real hero dashes on tracks and crawl in mud,
Fall down in despair or blow up by bombs,

記憶的碎片 Fragments of Memory

在地堡裡的將軍不關心的執行命令，
愚蠢的政客在辦公室裡掩藏。
他們僅計數獲得了多少枚獎牌，
或是佔領了多少個村莊及城鎮。

所有在*鳥巢*裡的歡呼都會消散，
在*立方水池*的波紋將最終變得平靜，
在新聞照相機消失在街頭，
運動員和訪客在他們回歸的飛行，
霧像神秘的帷幕也許再會降下，
比賽的記憶正像煙霧一樣的模糊，
那些可憐的受害者會有片刻的寧靜？

我看見壯觀的開幕和閉幕慶典，
及人類力爭優秀的精神，
他們在之間和諧地競爭，
為他們自己和他們國家的榮譽，
用他們血汗和耐力而不是子彈和槍杆，
她們在領獎中互相擁抱而她們的國家在戰爭，
或許人類還有和諧的希望。

2008年8月

*胡同:中國古老庭院

Generals carry-out orders indifferently in bunkers,
Thick-headed politicians hide in offices.
They count only how many medals they have won,
And how many villages and towns they have occupied.

All the uproars and hypes in the Bird Nest will fade,
Ripples in the Water Cube eventually become calm,
After the news-cameras vanish at the street corners,
The flood of athletes and visitors depart,
Fog probably will lower again like the mystic curtain,
Memory of the game is just as foggy as the smog,
Will those poor victims get a moment of calm?

I saw the spectacular opening and closing ceremonies,
The spirit of human beings striving for excellence,
They were competing harmoniously in-between,
For their own honors and for the their national glories,
With their sweat and endurance not bullets and guns,
Embracing on medal stand when their country is in war,
Perhaps there is hope for harmony in mankind.

Aug., 2008 Written during the 29th Olympic Game

*Hutongs: Ancient Chinese courtyards or alleys.

613　如果我醒不過來

如果我明天早晨沒有醒過來，
世界幾乎不會注意到我的缺席，
有些人也許惦念我的靈巧與存在，
其他的人甚而感覺減少點負擔。
小的發生攪動地方化的波紋，
人海將忽略較小的騷亂，

在那些對人品有敵意的暗殺以外，
我有做科學和教育家的光榮時代，
也有傷心的時刻與可悲失敗，
如今，在我老年，只希望做一位詩人，
您對我的預期如何評判並不重要，
我最大的勝利是釋放我頭腦的奴役，
只請求您的縱容讓我獨自生存。

人間有不同的形式去追求生活型態，
有些人以敗壞他們的對手為樂，
其他的不停的在舞池中扭轉或洗紙牌，
少數吸毒或者從街角去尋求樂趣，
還有許多人從瓶子裡得到解脫，
我以搬運文字、草木和土壤修造城堡，
來防衛緩慢和遲鈍的入侵。

我不是一位出色市民或是慘酷的惡棍，
在這個世界要非常有名或引人注目，
您必須是非常文明或是非常邪惡，
沒人會注意到您是守法者或是普通人。
雖然我從未是一位冒名騙子或叛徒，
我也不如聖賢的清真天使的無辜。

總而言之，我並不是一個如此的壞人，
我既未殺人又未放火，
我既不是大慈善家或人道主義者。
然而，我總是對這個行星保持忠誠，
離開我的地方比我來前更好一點，
並保持我一小片的地面綠色與肥沃。

613   **If I do not wake up**

If I do not wake up tomorrow morning,
The world will hardly notice my absence.
Someone may miss my handiness and presence,
And others may even feel fewer burdens.
Petite events stir only local ripples,
Easily overlook by the ocean of men.

Beyond those malicious personal assassinations,
I have my glorious days as a scientist and educator,
And heartbreak and shameful moment of defeat,
Now, at my rightful age, I merely wish to be a poet.
How you judge me is not vital in my prospective,
My greatest victory is to free my mental slavery,
And I only beg your indulgence to let me be me.

There are different forms pursuing lifestyles,
Some take pleasures to demoralize their rivals,
Others shuffle cards or twist on the dance floor,
A few smokes pot or seek pleasure from streets,
Then there are lots of people get relief from bottles,
I build my fortress by moving words, plants and soils,
In fending off the invasion of tardiness and dullness.

I am not an eminent citizen or atrocious villain,
To be very famous or noticeable in this world,
You will have to be either very civil or very evil,
No one ever notices you are law-abiding or ordinary.
Though I have never been an imposter or a traitor,
Nor am I sacred as a saint or innocent as an angel.

All in all, I am not such a bad fellow,
I have not caused anybody harm or murdered.
Nor am I a great philanthropist or a humanitarian,
Though, I am always loyal and faithful to Earth,
Leaving my place a bit better than before I came,
And keeping my patch of land green and fertile.

614　生命的透視

我覺得自己與樹上的葉子沒有不同,
經驗循環茂盛和死亡的命運,
只是我並不如小植物那樣的應變,
看它們自己進行季節性的更新,
我短暫存在的時光僅是一生一死,
不朽只是在字典裡的措辭。

一些相信是從前生的投胎,
其他的認為在死亡以後進入天堂,
但沒人能明確的預言未來,
他們都非常的微妙與無從捉摸,
像在微風裡的清煙,
好像幽靈的薄霧與風消散。

最長年齡的個體是宇宙,
它甚而有爆炸起點和最後的崩潰,
搏動的模型顯示它再次的復發,
一個週期與另一個完全獨立,
無可查出過去的證明或記憶,
在演變的宇宙復活是毫無意義。

我們不是生存在扁平或方形的社會,
以一個昏迷的頭腦和缺乏顧慮的幽默,
世界既不是透明也不是混濁,
您必須要有能力透視是非,
失敗而不知道您的缺點是不幸,
沒有努力的成功像在沙漠裡發現泉水,
運氣是偶然,勝利是瞬間的作為。

我不是一個非常出色或有口才的辯論家,
也不容易相信及受欺騙的熱誠者,
我對人類沒有巨大的禮物或貢獻,
總是為平凡及少有影響事物而吃力。
不跟隨我先驅者的腳步,
一點倔強又沒有足夠的謙卑,
一位典型恣意科學家的行為。

2008年8月27日

614   Life Perspectives

I see myself no different from leaves of a tree,
Experiencing cyclical flourishing and dying fate,
Except I am not as versatile as the tiny plants,
Seeing themselves go through seasonal rebirth,
My transient existence is once in a life time,
Immortality is only a definition in the dictionary.

Some believe reincarnation from previous life,
Others deem into heaven after death,
But no one can foretell the future with firmness,
They are all very intangible and elusive,
Like the tenuous smoke in the breezes,
Dissipates with wind as if phantom mists.

The longest entity is the age of the universe,
It even has an initial explosion and final collapse,
Pulsating model shows it recurring again and again,
One cycle is independent from another,
No past memory or evidence can be detected,
Resurrection is meaningless in an evolving cosmos.

We are not living in flat or square societies,
With an infatuated mind and lack prudent humor,
The world is neither transparent nor opaque,
You will have the ability to see through grey,
Failure without knowing your fault is unfortunate,
Effortless success likes finding a fountain in desert,
Luck is accidental and victory is transitory.

I am not a very colorful or articulate speaker,
Or an easy gullible enthusiast and ready believer,
I have no great contribution or gift to humanity,
Always sweat the trivial stuff with little impact.
Not follow my predecessors' innovative footsteps,
A bit stubborn and without humbleness,
A typical mentality belongs to a scientist's behavior.

Aug. 27, 2008

615　妄想趨勢

我們都假裝生活是很完善和正常，
又經常虛擬的好像別人行為。
我們對自己和別人都不真實，
用所有一切保存臉面而不是風格，
一個在經濟興旺社會的災害；
以一個傲慢和變態心理的看法，
錢能使鬼推磨和買得到愛。
不知道禮貌能說服而愛也許會失敗；
危險的境遇總是在勝利的境界。

世界把個別性混合進入一個熔爐，
妄想我們全部是繁榮和均等人才，
忽略他們的風俗，文化和宗教，
一些人只關心他們的市場和贏利，
其他的強制他們的觀點和重要性，
而忽視有些國家甚而沒有衛生設備，
還有那些狂熱宗教極端分子，
謀殺清白的人們而夢想不朽。

我也會做夢但並未去抹殺人類，
而在挪威首都接受諾貝爾獎杯，
但不知道獎是為什麼主題。
也未看見其他家人和受獎者，
大廳裡擠滿了死人包括愛因斯坦，
我不能肯定我是死了或是活，
在我的幻覺中有一個我真實的細節，
我不再是年輕英俊和活力充沛。

當我羞怯的接受獎品的時候，
它只是一塊無值得皺紋的紙張，
沒有字，沒有簽名沒有印章，
它包著我自己一隻手的紀念碑，
我拿的是我血淋淋沒有手指的胳膊。
在它消失之前我只有片刻的絕望，
當我醒過來坐在我的床邊，
完全的瓦解與十分令人的不安。
2008 年 8 月 30 日

615   Pretending Tendency

We are all pretending life is normal and great,
And often act fictitiously as if someone else.
We are untruthful to ourselves and to others,
Just to save face with all costs but not grace,
A calamity in an economic booming society;
With a view of arrogance and distorted mentality,
That rich can buy love or make ghosts to push mills.
Knowing not love may fail and courtesy will prevail;
The jaw of defeat is always at the verge of victory.

The world mixes individuality into a melting pot,
Think we are all equal in ability and prosperity,
Disregard their cultures, religions and customs,
Some care only their market shares and profits,
Others impose their views and values,
Ignore some countries don't even have facilities,
Then there are those fanatic religious extremists,
Murder innocents and dream to become immortality

I dream too not to obliterate the human race,
But to accept a Nobel Prize in Stockholm, Norway,
Yet did not know what subject that award was for,
Nor saw other recipients and their families,
The hall filled with dead people including Einstein,
I was not so certain that I am dead or still alive,
One detail from my real life was in my illusion,
I was no longer young and handsome with vitality.

By the time I timidly receive the prize,
It was only a piece worthless wrinkled paper,
No seals, no signatures and no words,
It wrapped around a trophy of my hand,
I was giving my own bloody arm without fingers,
I only had a moment of despair before it vanished,
I came awake and sat on the edge of my bed,
Utterly in devastation and drenching with dread.

Aug. 30, 2008

134　本質

我遊遍四海與大陸
廣而闊，
在曠野裡四從漫遊，
有如一隻小鳥一樣的自由，
我想像我能翻山，
過海，
也能克服無情的火災。

我曾自認，
是扭轉世界的動力，
但世界持續前進卻將我拋於天邊。

我一直在良善及正直中
勞動，
但是欺詐及蒙蔽，
卻污染我的智慧。

我的身軀包著血肉及筋骨，
我的行為，
被人的規則而約束。

我不能如我的願望
而生存，
也許死於不是我所希望。
如果你問我寧願如何，
我的答復不完全是由我自己。

我的所有及所無不很重要，
所有的我們都是空著手的離去。

2008 年 8 月

　　這是我個人的感觸，願望與一些人生不幸的遭遇。雖然我們都有某些渴望與期待，但是沒有任何人能操縱我們的命運。人生有一件事是無疑的，那就是沒有人能在他們離開這個世界的時候，帶走任何一點財物。

134   **Essence**

I travel oceans and continents
far and wide,
Strolling around in the open country,
And free as a bird,
My mind can climb the mountain
and cross the sea,
And overcome the fearful fire.

I thought I was the driving force
in turning the world.
But the world forges ahead leaves me behind.

I have labored
in the realms of righteous and integrity,
But swindle and deception
have tarnished my wit

My body encased by flesh and bones,
And my actions bounded
by the rules of men.

I cannot live the way as
I have wished for,
Perhaps die not the way as I would hope.
If you ask me what I would rather be,
The answer of mine is not totally up to me.

What I have and have not is not relevant,
For all of us will depart here with an empty hand.

August 2008

This is my personal feelings, opinions, wishes and some of the unfortunate encounters in life. Although we all have certain desire and expectation, but no one can have the total control of his life. One thing is certain, however, that no one can bring anything with him/her when they leave this world.

620 預期的改變

在一個遙遠土地的某處，
一個小村莊甚而沒有名字，
房子砌成的是土牆和稻草，
一個有名字的男孩但又無名，
他家住在一間小倉房卻很溫暖，
那是他品格滋養的來源。

從醒到睡然後從睡到醒，
他是有名有姓然後又成為無名，
如果他不能在日夜之間是他自己，
他怎能可以考慮他甚而是別人？
土地興旺天空無際，
沒人能阻止他有夢想。

戰爭和動亂把他載進混亂世界，
他在大學之前自讀與如何做人，
未能學到如何變得富有和成名，
但他有許多容忍的經驗，
半途插隊是更本不難，
所以他不是在當前社會的資產。

他只結婚一次不是那麼流行，
有幸或是不幸非他人能說，
老的婚姻取決於信念與緩和，
最容易走的路是採取不同方向，
他們吸進新妞或咳出老伴，
拋棄妻子就像丟掉破鞋。

人的頭腦和骨肉都是脆弱和易碎，
如果我們能直視美杜莎的眼睛，
而變成石頭沒有欺騙及痛苦，
或是請求宙斯授予我們力量和智慧。
在地球上我們不知道在哪裡找他們，
您只能去忍受你自己的悲哀。

2008 年 9 月 22 日

620 **Prospective Changing**

Somewhere in a faraway land,
A small village didn't even have a name,
Houses were built from adobe and straw,
A boy has a name yet nameless,
His family lived in a small barn but warm,
In character that was his source of nourishment.

Awake to sleep and sleep to awake,
He is someone then becomes no one,
If he can't be himself between day and night,
How can he even think about being someone else?
The land is thriving and the sky is unlimited,
No one can stop him having a dream.

War and turmoil carried him into a chaotic world,
He taught himself before colleges and be a man,
No help to others how to become rich and famous,
But with a lot of experience in endurances,
It is not hard to cut into the head of a line,
He is not a popular asset needed in current society.

He is not so modern that he only married once,
Fortunately or unfortunately is not for others to say,
Old marriage hinges on faith and conciliation,
The easier road is walking in different directions,
They breathe in new ones or cough out the old,
Disposing wife likes throwing away old shoes.

Human brain and flesh are flimsy and fragile,
If we could look straight into the eyes of Medusa,
And turn into stone without deception and pain,
Or ask Zeus to grant us wisdom and strength.
We do not know where to find them on earth,
You will just have to endure yourself.

Sept. 22, 2008

621　一盤棋賽的比喻

生命就像下棋，
我們僅是在比賽中的兵卒。
我們的途徑不是由我們自己的選擇，
而是一個下棋人的決策，
勝負全由統盤性的設計，
我們根據命運直奔或是斜爬。

在複雜的交戰之下，
我們可以被我們的敵人消滅，
由錯誤的死亡不是罪惡，
由戰略策劃的死亡才是很殘忍，
身體相似是棋子，
頭腦做決定身體服從。

為了最後勝利的宗旨，
我們為別人成功而犧牲。
當主角在戰場上前後左右奔馳，
我們只能逐步向前移動，
如果我們在屠殺中辛存，
最後的結果將是我們的化身

世界像似密林一樣的預謀，
偽裝掠食動物的陷井，
慎密的行動像計劃一樣的迫切，
錯誤最後的結論是死亡，
誰能去拯救淪落的女皇？
只有兵卒的勝利才是贖身者.

國王僅是在階層的一個傀儡，
像現代民主制度的總統，
一個權威性的木偶與無力的個體，
被那些愚蠢的夥伴而圍攏，
他們能破壞我們的生計和聲望，
和震動世界財務與經濟。

2008 年 9 月 24 日

621   Chess Game Analogy

Life is like playing chess,
We are only pawns in the game.
Our paths are not by our own choice,
But by actions of the chess master,
Winning or losing is by the grand design,
We dash or crawl according to destiny.

In the intricate engagements,
We can be annihilated by our enemy,
Death by a blunder is not as evil,
Death by a calculated strategy is malice.
Body is similar to a chess piece,
Mind makes a decision and body obeys.

For the final objective of victory,
We are sacrificed for others to succeed.
While the potent players zip around on stage,
We can only move step by step never to retreat,
If we survive slaughter by our opponent,
The final outcome will be our embodiment.

The world is as malicious as a jungle,
Traps are camouflaged by the predators,
Prudent motion is just as imperative as planning,
The ultimate conclusion of an error is death,
Only the victory of a pawn is the redeemer,
Who else could resurrect downfall of the queen?

The king is only a figurehead in the hierarchy,
Like presidents in the modern democracy,
Surrounded by those imprudent cronies,
A bunch of self-centered and conceited dummies,
Yet they can ruin our livelihood and prestige,
And shake the world finance and economy.

Sept 24, 2008

622　象徵性的觀點

我們不是在野外不穿衣服的野獸，
也不是在森林狩獵為生的野蠻者，
我們不去耕作因功而得收穫，
容易取得造成我們變得懶散，
稀罕造成空虛及不安全。

我們全都播種了幾顆種子，
不管它們是核、想法或單詞，
沒人充分的能根除我們播種。
我們的種植也許會結果實，
枯萎的花草歸結於我們忽略，
荒廢的土地將是被荒廢。

我們知道葉子是從樹枝發芽，
但經常接受歪曲事實的預言，
植物彌漫香味但不能發言，
他們有自然的能力去表示感覺，
我寧可聞到他們的氣味和清真，
而不聽人的胡言亂語。

我們從不考慮我們喝的水，
我們吃的食物是否是安全。
我們的慾望淹沒我們的評斷，
縱容克服我們的警惕，
我們的舌頭將品嘗酸或甜，
只有腸胃比我們的意志要聰明，
它不僅是為我們的安全並為存活保衛。

我是我過去外觀的一部分，
但脫換了我多半的天真與外殼，
我與野花沒有不同，
有開花與興旺的期間，
也有凋殘和退色的時候。

2008 年 10 月 2 日

622 Symbolic View

We are not beasts in the wild naked,
Nor savages in the jungle hunting for prey,
We do not cultivate to merit harvest,
Easy accessibility induces our laziness,
Scarcity creates insecurity and emptiness.

We all have sowed a few seeds in life,
Whether they are pits, words or ideas,
No one can root-out what we have spread.
What we have planted may bear fruits,
Withered plants are due to our neglect,
Wasted land will be laid waste.

We know leaves bud from branches of a tree,
But often accept the distorted prophet,
Plants permeate perfumes but no voices,
Their natural abilities to express,
I rather smell their scents and innocence,
Not listen to Man's gibberish and nonsense.

We never think about the water we drink,
Foods we eat and whether they are safe.
Our desires overwhelm our judgment,
Indulgence overcomes our alertness
Our tongue will taste sour or sweet,
Only stomach is wittier than our will,
It guards our safety not just survivability.

I am a part of my past in facade,
But shed most of my naiveness and scales.
I am no different from the wild flowers,
There is a period of prosperous and blossom,
And there is time to wither and to fade.

Oct. 2, 2008

623　變體的差距

霜幾天前就來了，
以後天氣又變得溫和，
柔軟的微風是相當的誘人，
誰會相信冬天就要來臨呢？
大自然就像所有的母親，
變化莫測的改變她的喜怒哀樂。

綠葉變黃然後又變鮮紅，
像蝴蝶一樣在秋天空氣裡飛舞，
旋轉揮動勉強的告別，
季節性的變形是嚴酷的現實，
您會在下一個春天更加可愛的回歸，
但沒人可說我會在哪兒。

我們都是地球上的居民，
我由誕生而是一個國家的公民，
又由選擇採納另一個國度，
您是一個全球羨慕的種類，
我普通的像一粒沙漠裡的沙，
除了我有身分和智慧。

我們的福利不像樹那樣的悠閒，
我所說、所為或所寫都可能致命，
處方比描述更加有方針。
其中一個錯誤僅是誤解，
別的錯誤也許導致死亡，
在評斷中的冒險乃是嚴重危害。

您從容的在風中飛舞，
我們勞動，我們為生活積累財富，
擁有浩大的物質資產，
但每次只能使用一件，
只活一生又不能帶走任何財產，
然後我們不再會有另一個春天。

2008 年 10 月 11 日

623   **Disparity in Metamorphosis**

    Frost came a few days ago
    Weather became balmy after,
    Soft breeze is rather seductive,
    Who would think winter is near?
    Mother Nature is kindly like all mothers,
    Unpredictably change her mood.

    Green leaves turn to yellow then red,
    Flutter like butterflies in the autumn air,
    Twirl and wave farewell reluctantly,
    Seasonal metamorphosis is harsh reality,
    Your return next spring even lovelier,
    Where I will be no one can say,

    We are all residents of Earth,
    I am a citizen of a country by birth,
    And adopt another nation by choice,
    You are a universally envied species,
    I am ordinary like a grain of sand in the desert,
    Except I have an identity and intellect.

    Our well-being is not as leisure as trees,
    What we say, do or write could be fatal,
    Prescription is more directive than description,
    Error in one only a misunderstanding,
    Error in the other may cause death,
    The peril in judgment is very lethal.

    You are leisurely dancing in the wind,
    We labor our life to accumulate wealth,
    Own vast riches and materials ,
    But can only use one thing at a time,
    Live one life and carry nothing when we go,
    There will be no spring for us afterwards.

Oct. 11, 2008

625 振奮的顏料

一個充滿活力 的少女，
堅固的腹部合適的乳房，
暴露她的腹股溝和肚臍眼，
洋溢她的年輕和芬芳，
誰能抵抗這樣魅力和引誘？
我也不是一塊沒有感覺石頭。

我以前看過這些閃電的攻勢，
但由於生存需要的壓服，
又太怯懦而未能玩年輕人的遊戲，
我被浸在奮鬥中間，
讓旋渦掃走了我的年青，
骨肉的濫用必須要等它的時辰。

我現在非常休閒的生活，
眼睛大開的去窺視又有足夠的時間，
我所看見的圖像不在我的世紀，
激蕩人心的音樂已經失調，
我在他們的聲調之後數十年，
我所能感覺的並不是論點。

我曾經有我的機會和振奮，
雖然我們不能在街道同一邊走路，
或者在同個入口進入劇院，
黑暗如天堂般的是我們安慰。
那是模糊不清又是太久以前，
但是記憶仍然是哀痛又很甜蜜。

在我們的世代我們仍是幸運，
自由戀愛正開始開花，
與少許大膽與很多決心，
我們克服了傳統的障礙。
在情況掌握的之外，
我們也十分放縱和沉溺。

2008 年 10 月 31 日

625 **Pigments of Elation**

A vibrant and vivacious maiden,
With fitting breasts and firm abdomen,
Exposing her groin and belly button,
Permeating youthfulness and fragrance,
Who can resist such allure and appeal?
I am not a piece of stone without feel.

I have seen all these blitzes before,
But overwhelmed by the call for existence,
And too timid to play the youthful game,
I was submerged in the middle of struggle.
And let the whirlpool swept away my youth.
Exploitation of flesh must wait for its turn.

I am now living in a very leisurely way,
Eyes wide open to peep and time to spare,
The picture I see is not in my epoch,
The melody of swing is out of tune,
I am decades behind their stanza.
What I can feel is beside the point.

I had my chance and elation,
We could not walk on the same side of the road,
Or enter a theater at the same entrance,
Darkness was our heavenly solace.
That was just too fuzzy and too long ago,
But memory is still sweet as well as sorrow.

We were the luckier ones in our generation,
Free courtship was beginning to bloom,
With a little daring and a lot of determination,
We overcame the obstacles of tradition.
Beyond the clutch of circumstances,
We too indulged with extravagance.

Oct. 31, 2008

626　一絲微風

第一次季節性冬雪來訪，
我幾乎還未完成清除秋天的落葉，
季節是非常不仁慈和無情，
植物和花草都逃不過她的鞭打，
他們沒有聲音但可以表白情緒，
瀰漫芳香是他們天生的才能。

我們與那些野花沒有不同，
有興旺和開花的期間，
有凋枯和退色隱沒的時刻。
世界對人與畜牲是一個冷酷，
最冷的地方是宇宙的虛無，
學習它也傳染了我冷淡的態度。

我耗費了整個成人沉溺在乾坤，
丟掉人的胡言亂語在遙遠距離，
在喧鬧和吵鬧的狀態之下，
我甚而聽不見我自己的心聲，
我寧可去飽賞山頂上的夜風，
而不損失我自己真實接觸的意味。

由於職業隔離的危害，
我發現了許多物體但不是夥伴，
享受詩詞及悠閒的飲茶並不流行，
漫長無眠夜訓練了我的耐力，
在黑暗中啼哭不是我們這一類，
我們只是流汗與流血而不是眼淚。

我們全都在貧富之間掙扎，
不管您是富裕的或是貧窮，
您的擁有總是沒有界限，
基本的區別是您的自滿。
直到一天年齡取代了您的熱誠，
您生命中佔據不再被重視。

2008年11月7日

626   A Wisp of Freeze

First seasonal snow has paid its visit,
I barely finished sweeping away the leaves,
The season is very unkind and merciless,
Plants and flowers cannot escape her whip,
They have no voices yet have their expression,
Permeating scents are their natural instincts.

We are not so different from the wild flowers,
There is a period of prosperity and blossom,
And there is time to wither or fade into absence.
The world is a cold place for Man and beasts,
The coldest place is the void of the universe,
Studying it has infected me with the frostiness.

I spent entirely adult life to indulge cosmos,
And left Man's nonsense in far-off distance,
In the gibberish noisy and rowdiness,
I can't even hear what I think,
I rather enjoy the mountain fresh night air,
Not lose the sense of contact truly myself.

With the hazards of professional isolation,
I found many bodies but not buddies,
Enjoying poetry and sipping tea are not prevalent,
Long sleepless nights taught me endurance.
Crying in the darkness is not in our species,
We only shed sweat and blood not tears.

We all struggle between rich or poor,
No matter you are in poverty or affluent,
There is no limit in what you possess,
The basic difference is your self-content.
Until one day that age has claimed your zest,
What you hold in life is no longer deemed.

Nov. 7, 2008

627 情操的魔力

吸收陽光、空氣和水，
自然創造生存形狀的個體，
我們稱它為光合作用。
它淨化我們的空氣及滋養我們的植物，
養育綠葉青枝、水果及五穀，
我們然後製造食品和釀酒。
不關它是草食或肉食動物，
我們全都受益它的恩愛。

我在夜空研究遙遠的星辰，
但愚蠢的忽略了附近的星光，
我太粗俗的接觸柔軟的骨肉，
寧可掌握冷硬的金屬，
只有貓頭鷹和蝙蝠才是我的訪客。
我崇拜的對象很遙遠而不實用，
又沒有找到任何外星人，
只有幾個巨星有鋇反常的現象*。

我就像任何人珍惜晴天，
但仍然習慣性的張望夜間的黑暗，
我不是在夜色薄霧裡尋花，
也不是尋找我長期忠誠的香果，
如果您沒有什麼尋求和竊取，
寧靜的夜晚是很清白又無混雜，
我過去沒有一點功勳去歡呼，
只有寫甜蜜詩詞來溫暖我的心腸。

我尚未學到我的訓誡，
又未能深思常久而成聖人。
幽默是很容易進入頭條新聞，
我甚而不可能羨慕普通的押韻。
我堅強鼓舞我的情緒，
我的虛榮是自我陶醉，
現實就像真理和陽光一樣的純淨，
憤世嫉俗僅是自製的規範。

*在紅色巨星中發現所謂鋇元素反常現象建議它與理論不合。

627   **The Alchemy of Sentiment**

Assimilating sunshine, water and air,
Nature creates living entities of shapes,
We call it the process of photosynthesis.
It purifies our air and nourishes our plants,
Nurtures our greens, fruits and grains,
We then create dishes and wines.
It matters not herbivores or carnivores,
We all have benefited by its kindness.

I studied distant stars in the night sky,
But foolishly neglected the nearby starlight,
I was too coarse to touch soft fleshy tissues,
Rather handle the cold and hard metals,
Only owls and bats were my visitors.
I worshiped objects too far to be practical,
But did not find any little green men,
Only a few giants have an anomaly of barium*.

I cherish sunny days like anybody else,
But still look into the dark night as a habit,
I search not flowers in the nocturnal mist,
Nor fruits for my long loyal fidelity,
Quiet night is untainted and sincere,
If you have nothing to seek and steal.
There is little merit to cheer my past,
Only write sweet verses to warm my heart.

I have not yet learned my lessons,
Or meditated long enough to be a saint,
Humors are easier to get into headlines,
I can't even envy the ordinary rhymes.
I adamantly invigorate my sentiment,
My vanity is my own narcissism,
Reality is as pure as truth and sunshine,
Cynicism is only self-made paradigm.

*A so-called Abundance Anomaly discovered in the element of barium in red-giants suggests it violates the norm.

628　吳牛喘月

一絲飄渺在藍天的雲彩,
一陣吹來微風的芬芳,
我感覺非常的舒適與美妙,
除了那些不合情理的落葉要掃除。
體諒這不是損傷到您的樂趣,
但都市裡的人卻不能有如此的榮幸。

我看不見他們是在追逐什麼,
為汙濁的空氣,嘈雜聲和傳染病,
華麗的服裝和半暴露的乳房,
或者是在肢體和大腿之間的黏液,
一人的慾望是另一個人的冒險,
您的尋求不一定是您的願望。

在明顯感覺的誘惑之外,
帶來是隱瞞的欺騙,
與掩藏的操縱和貪婪,
在激流社會根深蒂固的編織,
要成功那裡總是有犧牲,
新鮮空氣與平靜環境並不便宜。

無意義的修辭現在全已吹過,
勝者或敗者都停止了他們爭吵。
穿著與年齡無所爭執,
選擇的因素不是膚色與種族,
競選諾言像是便宜的胡說八道,
全球性暖化仍是全球性熱的論點,
惡化環境並不引起任何人的苦惱。

不要責備他們的放肆,
我們應該負責他們的傲慢。
銀行業的危機和房地產拒斥,
失業率上升而市場貶值,
如果您進一步看過太平洋,
腐敗的前任總統都在監獄,
我們僥倖的看見我們的,消失以朦朧。

2008 年 11 月 16 日

628   A Gasping Bull

A wispy cloud in the blue sky,
A puff of fragrance in the breeze,
I am feeling immensely easy and tidy,
Except raking of the bloody falling leaves.
Consider this as not detrimental to your jolly,
But a privilege not offered by a metropolis.

I do not see what they are chasing about,
For filthy air, loud noise and infectious diseases,
Flashy garments and half exposed breasts,
Or the slimy texture between limbs and legs?
One man's desire is another man's peril,
What you wish may not be what you seek.

Beyond the obvious sense of seductions,
Come with the concealing dishonesty,
And the hidden manipulation and greed,
The fabric rooted in a fast-moving society.
There are always sacrifices to be successful,
Tranquil mindset and fresh air are not cheap.

Now the meaningless rhetoric has blown over,
Winners or losers ceased their bickering.
There are no disputes about wardrobes or ages,
Skin color has not been relevant in races,
The campaign promises are as cheap as shit,
Global warming is still a global hot issue,
Deteriorating environment causes no one's irk.

Do not blame them for their presumptuousness,
We are responsible for their loftiness,
Banking in crises and housing in jeopardy,
Unemployment rise and markets descend.
If you look further across the Pacific Ocean,
Corrupted former presidents are in custody,
We are fortunate to see ours fade into secrecy.

Nov. 16, 2008

629　微不足道的 詩

科學家必須述說真理，
除了錯誤、缺點和自負，
詩人能創造山水及溪谷，
精采的陽光和淒涼消沈的意氣，
您必須要瞭解他們的內在的含義。

我能看得出為什麼詩人值得敬慕，
他們使用措辭建造宇宙，
而科學家們在黑暗的地牢裡隱藏，
用儀器、圖表及公式，
經常與失敗和寂寞鬥爭。

我們的頭很小但又非常厚實，
宇宙很浩大但又很稀薄，
他們兩者世界都是相同構成，
沒有約制、沒有極限也沒有界限，
他們製造想像力和自由的意志。

我們沒有規則去比文字與紅磚，
它們都是建設城堡的要素，
一個是為想像一個是為現實，
只要目標是無辜和高尚，
你的責任僅是忠於職守。

作家熱愛寫作不一定是因為內容，
一些為了激情其他是為了報酬，
多數守衛他們的榮譽和思想意識，
尚有少數背叛他們的原則及正直，
我為解放我內在的空間而寫作。

我有那種特權品嘗兩個範例，
是偶然與激情但不是設計，
我有責任保護兩者領域，
沉重的負擔束縛我的雙手，
我既不是怪科學家也不是狂詩人。

2008 年 11 月 25 日

629   **Poetic of Nothingness**

What scientists say has to be truth,
Except for errors, flaws and arrogance,
A poet can create mountains and valleys,
Brilliant sunshine and dreary despair,
You will have to decipher their inner state.

I can see why poets are adorable,
They build a universe using words,
While the scientists hide in dark dungeons,
With apparatus, graphs and equations,
Constantly battling with defeat and loneliness.

Our head is so small yet it is very thick,
The universe is huge but thin and sparse ,
They are two worlds of self-same constructs,
No restrictions, no limits and no boundaries,
They produce imaginations and free wills.

There is no rule to equal a word to a brick,
They are the essences in erecting a citadel,
One is for idea and other for the reality,
As long as the goal is innocent and noble,
The accountability is attentive to one's duty.

Writers love to write not because of content,
Some for passion and others for reward,
Most guard their honor and ideology,
A few betray their principle and integrity,
I write to release the flood of my inner space.

I have the luxury to taste both paradigms,
By accident and passion not by design,
I have the responsibility to defend both realms,
Heavy burdens constrain my free hands,
I am neither a nutty poet nor a mad scientist.

Nov. 25, 2008

630　老年醫學之外

我們都擔心皺紋與老化，
然而，他們象徵成年與智慧，
生活經驗塑造了我們的門面，
好運贈送了我們長壽，
那些不幸的人居住在小山邊。
有些社會尊敬年齡是神聖的象徵，
我們對待年老好像破鞋子一樣冷漠。

我們對老年的認識只是膚淺，
外表上的衡量要比內在有分量。
我們經常的在修改我們的表面，
用唇膏、面霜和頭髮漂白。
那些奢侈者也許臉部拉皮，
捲褶肚皮及增大乳房，
欺騙自然是不合乎清理的徒然。

年齡的進化是自然的進展，
驕傲的英雄一般死於年青，
傻子們卻能活到老年。
悲傷的現實是為那些早死的人，
那裡不會再有其他精采的日出。
天堂裡是否有壯觀的日落？
那就讓問題去做回答。

當代的人們被小機件而侵佔，
沒有人會聽見老人的呻吟，
您不妨對天空詛咒或對樹林呼喊，
星星是如此的遙遠很難聽見你，
樹林雖然很近但是並不反對，
聽見您自己的回聲著實是很愉快，
或者您總是可以去老人中心找到安慰。

2008 年 11 月 27 日

630   **Beyond Geriatrics**

We are fearful of wrinkles and old age.
Yet, they symbolize wisdom and maturity.
Life experiences shaped our facade,
Good fortune bestowed longevity,
Those unfortunates are residing on the hills.
Some cultures respect age as a sacred emblem,
We treat ours as if old shoes, indifferently.

Our knowledge of aging is only skin deep,
Exterior weights more than interiors.
We constantly modify our appearances,
By lipstick, facial powder and dyeing hair,
Those extravagant ones may have face-lift,
Tummy-tuck and breast augmentations,
Deceiving Mother Nature is un-motherly vain.

Age progression is a natural advancement,
Proud ones are generally dying young,
The foolish bunch departs in a rightful age.
The sad reality for those who died early,
There will be no more brilliant sunrise.
Is there any magnificent sunset in heaven?
Let the question be the answer.

This generation overwhelms by gadgets,
No one hears the groaning of elderly,
You might as well curse sky or shout to trees,
Stars are remote and take ever to hear you,
Trees are nearby but do not speak back.
Hearing your own echo is truly comfort,
Or you can always go to Senior Center to find solace.

Nov. 27, 2008

631　半真假的傷心

在我們靜脈裡的血液不多，
在我們的眼皮下的淚花有限。
如果我們為無意義的發生大事浪費，
他們會很快的被排泄而用盡，
我們然後就變成貧血和無情的吸血鬼。

當我們需要熱血去抵抗疾病，
或者淚水沖洗我們真正的悲傷，
我們無血可流與無眼淚可落。
沒有什麼比偽造哀痛更尷尬，
我們然後就比男女演員更低劣。

我們為我們死掉的寵物而痛哭，
但砍倒了一顆樹幾乎沒有感動，
他們都是生化裡生命的個體。
我們不去踢狗而經常對樹方便，
由於狗會咬人而樹是惰性。

我們有多少人抱歉踩死螞蟻？
但是，死亡是死亡，光彩或卑賤，
在任何情況下它們全無意義，
完全的一致，但每件不同，
悲傷是悲傷，你的或者螞蟻。

我看木材爐子裡的火焰舞蹈，
水壺軟軟的嘶嘶響及歌頌，
在荒涼和冷寒的冬天早晨，
溫暖安慰我的感覺和筋骨，
柴火是更加無辜和富於情感。

我沒有開燈或電視機，
害怕把有造化的調和嚇跑，
我從未為砍樹而流淚，
亦不覺得遺憾燒它們的手腿，
我並不比那些伐木工人友善。

2008 年 12 月 1 日

631   **Pseudo Bleeding Heart**

There is only so much blood in our veins,
And a limited amount of tears under our eyelids.
If we shed them lavishly for insignificant stuff,
Soon they will be exhausted and drained dry,
We then turn into anemic and heartless vampires.

When we need hot blood to fight diseases,
Or tears to wash away our true sadness,
We have no blood to bleed nor tears to shed.
There is nothing worse than faked sorrow,
We are then inferior to actresses and actors.

We cry passionately for the passing of our pet,
But hardly have any emotion felling down a tree,
They are both living entities in biochemistry.
We don't kick a dog but often piss on trees,
Dog knows how to bite but trees are inert.

How many of us regret stepping on an ant?
But, death is death, trivial or grand,
They are meaningless in whatever circumstance,
Utterly same, yet different in each case,
Sadness is sadness, yours or ants.

I watch flames dancing in my woodstove,
Water kettle softly sizzles and chants,
In a bleak and chilly winter morning,
Warmth soothes my bones and my feelings,
Wood fire is more innocent and affectionate.

I did not turn on lights or television set,
Afraid to scare away the blissful harmony,
I never shed tears as I hack the trees,
Nor feel regret to burn their arms and legs,
I am no better than those lumberjacks.

Dec. 1, 2008

632　一個普通人

我不勝有名，但是人，
你很容易看見我可見的部分，
我的品德、精神和思路卻被隱沒。
我並不富裕但也不貧窮，
只是一位在時列車上的乘客，
攜帶很少需要的行李，
來去都是空著雙手，
單獨在月臺上當列車離去。

我全心的與朋友分享，
但從不浪費心力去討好任何人，
我寧可與我的家犬坐在樹下，
享受他們無辜沈默和忠誠。
僅是與任何人為友，
它就像與敵人飲茶，
您不能肯定什麼在杯子之後，
亦不能說明茶葉子的真實性。

我們總是把一切如同應該，
旋轉一個龍頭那裡有水，
按動開關那裡有電，
要求補賞那裡就是補貼，
接受不到的，我們就去竊取及搶奪。
我們為需要祈禱上帝，
當神沒有回復我們的要求，
我們然後懷疑他們是否存在。

我們希望奇蹟來解決我們的問題，
但奇蹟是罕有而現實是現實，
時間比白日夢更可靠，
容忍是賢良耐心是能力。
希望是海市蜃樓而我們全都依賴，
未實現的願望會使我們更加忿怒，
如果不成功我們然後就詛咒所有人。
噢!多麼美妙!
如果您沒有任何需求。

2004年12月4日

632   **A Common Man**

I am nobody, yet somebody,
It is easy to see the visible part of me,
But not my virtue, spirit and mentality,
I am neither wealthy nor in poverty,
Only a passenger on the train of time,
Carrying very little baggage of need,
Arriving and departing with hands zilch,
Alone on the platform when the train leaves.

I share with friends whole heartedly,
But do not waste effort to court just any man,
I would rather sit under a tree with my dog,
Enjoy their innocence and loyalty.
Just to have anyone to be friend with,
It's like sipping tea with the enemy,
You can't be certain what's behind the cup,
Nor tell the authenticity of the tea-leafs.

We always take everything for granted,
Turning a faucet on, there is water,
Flipping a switch, there is electricity,
Demand a handout and there is subsidy,
Fail to receive, we just grab and steal.
We pray to gods for whatever we need,
When divinities do not answer our calls,
We doubt whether they have ever existed.

We hope for miracles to solve our problems,
But miracles are rare and reality is realistic,
Time is more dependable than daydreams,
Tolerance is virtue and patience is ability.
Hopes are mirages but we all rely on them,
Unfulfilled wishes only get us angrier,
We then curse everyone if don't succeed.
Oh! How wonderful!
If you have nothing to seek.

Dec. 4, 2004

637　鄉愁

我從江北來,
那裡是窮鄉僻壤,
土牆茅屋,
簡陋的門窗,
擋不住寒風,
卻有家庭的溫暖。

我從江南去,
光陰不斷的流逝,
人屋全非,
我無處搜尋我的幼年,
與甜美快活的年華,
只有那些失落回憶。

回到過去是沒有可能,
唯一途徑是勇往向前,
智慧和力量是我唯一的工具,
創意是自己承擔的才能,
帶者學到的知識與技術,
收穫是來自血汗與容忍。

我居住他鄉,
有家與舒適房舍,
和一個簡單鄉村生活,
耕種一小塊土地,
外地人居住他鄉,
卻有自足的感覺。

2001 年 11 月於台南

637   **Nostalgia**

I came from north of the river,
There were poor and barren,
Grass huts and adobe walls,
Crude windows and doors,
They cannot stop the bitter cold,
Yet, my home was affectionate and warm.

I returned home from south of the river,
Time has haplessly elapsed,
Face changed and house demolished,
I could neither find my childhood,
Nor sweet carefree youth,
Only those lost memories.

There is no way back to the past,
Only avenue is moving forward,
Strength and wit are my only tools,
Ingenuity is self-imposed talent,
With the knowledge and skill I have acquired,
Harvest comes with sweat and endurance.

I reside in a foreign country,
Having a warm and comfortable home,
And a simple and country life,
Cultivating a small plot of soil,
A foreigner lives in an alien land,
With a feeling of self-content.

Nov. 2001 in Tainan, Taiwan

635　年尾的回顧

假日可以是歡悅也能是哀傷，
那要取決於誰在描繪圖像。
光陰從宇宙的貯藏中湧出，
像似在狹窄河裡急流的流水，
而兩邊河岸只是供給風光。
我們數下降的秒鐘來迎接新的時代，
所有新年決議就像煙火一樣的一閃，
舊年就像溜走的死亡。

節日不是說教哲學的時候，
然而，生死就像新年一樣的平常。
新生帶給我們喜悅，新希望與展望，
死亡剝去了我們的私下又結束一章，
我們肌體受限精神自由的像薄霧一樣，
我們不能阻止陌生人張望我們的裸體，
垂死不是我們的過失而是自然的安排，
它不可避免;我們不應該感到歉然。

至於我在地球表面上一小片土地，
我一直如我自己像老傻瓜一樣的愉快，
夢想不是我的特長，
我情願棄權去好好的睡一覺。
醒來之後帶著新希望
啊!我但願有一杯奇蹟的振奮劑 - 咖啡，
來清洗我的朦朧及帶我回到實在。

我沒有花言巧語的才能，
也不是有想像力畫家的或詩人，
當所有英勇者向前猛衝，
血氣旺盛的成年固化他們興旺，
而貧窮者只能天天謀圖維生。
我不屬於他們任何那一類，
只是離開我那美好的以往，
看著我的沙漏不停的漏光。

635   A Year-end Reflection

Holidays can be joyous and can be sad,
It depends upon who is painting the picture.
Time gushes out from the cosmic reservoir,
It flows like rapids in the narrow river,
And the riverbanks provide only scenery.
We count-down seconds to see a new era,
All resolutions flash by as if fireworks,
The yesteryear slips away like death.

It is not the time to preach philosophy in festivity,
Yet, birth and death is routine as the New Year.
Birth brings us joys, new hopes and prospects,
Death ends a chapter and strips away our privacy.
Our spirit is free as mist but body restricted,
We cannot stop strangers to see us naked,
Dying is not our fault but natural arrangements,
It is inevitable; we should not be very apologetic.

As far as been myself on surface of the earth,
I was happy as an old fool like my usual self,
Dream is not my specialty,
I would gladly to yield for a good night nap.
It brings back a new prospect after waking up.
O! I wish I have cup of the miracle drug – coffee,
Wash off my mistiness and give back my reality.

I am not very articulate in expression,
Nor an imaginative poet or painter,
While all the courageous ones thrust forward,
The strong ones solidify their prosperities,
And the poor only try to survive day by day.
I do not belong to any of these masses,
Only moving away from my wondrous past,
Watching sands in my hourglass deplete away.

在一個真實推論的狀態，
我們的存在並不是想像。
生命從一章推進到另一章節，
您幾乎不能預言什麼是下頁。
預測性不是定性或定量的兩者之一，
我既不會調解也不會挑撥。
稱讚或譴責是利他主義，
乞求您瞭解我不是我的目標。

世界把個別性混合變得含糊，
忽略他們的文化，皮膚顏色與差異，
認為他們是在道德和能力全是均等。
一些人只關心他們的市場份額和贏利，
其他的強加他們的理想和意圖，
還有那些狂熱宗教極端分子，
謀殺清白的人而高呼神很偉大，
真理僅是在現實中幻覺的碎片。

我感覺我已履行義務和滿足，
既無憂慮工作保障或失業。
我沒有多少儲蓄也未負債，
只是欠我自己想盡力的滿腔熱忱。
你能僅僅料想在這個暗淡的期間，
我們甚有福氣能繼續的爭取。
幸運或不幸都有相等的蓋然性，
我們是那培養愉快一年的主宰。

2008 年 12 月 28 日

In a pragmatic state of deduction,
Our existences are not imaginations.
Life pushes on from chapter to chapter,
You can hardly tell what's on the next page.
Predictability is either qualitative or quantitative,
I am neither conciliatory nor provocative.
Commendation or condemnation is altruistic,
Begging you to understand me is not my aim.

The world blends individuality into ambiguity,
Ignores their cultures, skin-colors and diversities,
Thinks they are all equal in morality and ability.
Some only care their market shares and profits,
Others impose their views and dogmatic ideals,
Then there are those fanatic religious extremists,
Murder innocents and shout god is great,
Truth is only a fragment of illusion in reality.

I am sensibly fulfilled and contented,
Nor worry about joblessness or job security.
I don't have much savings or bear any debts,
Only owe myself the eagerness to do my best.
Just to think in this bleak period of time,
We are blessed for our continuous endeavors.
Fortunate or unfortunate has an equal probability,
We are the one to cultivate a Happy New Year.

Dec. 28, 2008

三． 新的開始

知覺是領悟的橋梁，
沒有它我們是在恍惚蒙昧。
良心是公正的城堡，
缺乏它造成我們根基腐壞。
…
以人類的機智與才幹，
我們可以把世界弄得光彩，
在藝術、音樂、詩歌、科學和氣概，
創造一個為愛與和平更美好的所在，
直到我們的頭髮變白皮膚皺起來。

III · New Beginning

Consciousness is a bridge to awareness,
Without it we are in a state of trance.
Conscience is the citadel to righteousness,
Lack of it leads us to the corruptive base.
…
With the ingenuity and talent of the human race,
We could make the world more glorious,
In art, music, poetry, science and spirit,
Creating a better place for peace and love,
Until our skin wrinkles and hair turns white.

636　我所看見的新年

寒風在我的門外咆哮,
冰雪霏霏的落在我的窗臺,
窗戶遮風板激烈的動搖與號叫,
如果您想這是二零零九歡迎的信號,
我不知道這是一個非常好的預兆。

彩球在時代廣場下降,
秒鐘計數下降到零秒。
這不是像切一片蛋糕那麼明確,
新年與舊年在一起纏繞,
我們激動的叫它是元旦。

嚴寒沒有阻止在街上的興致,
我在我溫暖床上歡迎新的開始,
其他地方早已向舊年說告別,
還有其他那些為它的來臨而等待,
時間幾小時不是永恆而是人造。

計時法是人為的方案,
水從桶裡一點一滴的漏下,
鐘擺在大廳裡反覆的搖擺,
地球的公轉和自轉有如計時器,
在這裡的一秒不是在那裡的一秒。

天日的劃分為小時, 幾分和幾秒
僅是根據我們生活方式和癖好,
時間在我們的宇宙不能倒退,
然而, 那裡有足夠的時間發送資訊,
到居住在西邊朋友的舊年。

生活很苛刻並且足夠令人可怕,
戰爭在世界的其他角落爆發,
我們設法找每個可能的時機,
慶祝是為了舉行儀式而慶祝,
不管它是快樂時光或是苦澀悲哀。

2009 年 1 月 1 日

636   **A New Year as I see it**

Cold wind is howling outdoors,
Snow and ice spit on my windowsills,
Shutters rattle violently and windows whistle,
If you think this is a welcome sign of 2009,
I do not know if this is a very good omen.

The ball has descended in Times Square,
Number of seconds counted-down to zero.
It was not clean-cut like a slice of cake,
The young and old year intertwined together,
We only impulsively call it a New Year.

Bitter freeze didn't dampen spirit in the streets,
I welcomed a new beginning in my warm bed,
Others said farewell to it somewhere else,
Then there are others still waiting for its arrival,
Hours of time are artificial at best not eternal.

Time-keeping is a manmade scheme,
Water drips drop by drop from a pail,
Pendulum swings back and forth in a hall,
Or by the revolutions and rotations of the earth,
One second here does not equal to a second there.

The division of a day, hour, minute or second,
Is according only to our lifestyle and habit,
Time is not reversible in our universe,
Yet, there is still time enough to send a message,
To friends who reside west of us in the old year.

Life is harsh and dreadful enough,
Wars erupted in other corners of the world,
We try to find every possible occasion,
Celebrating is for the sake of celebration,
Regardless, it is a happy hour or bitter sorrow.

Jan. 1, 2009

638 沒有形式的生命

沒有形式的生命乃是玄學，
存在可以是精神、靈魂或骨肉，
可見與不可見僅是介質的幻覺，
有形或無形不同的是在描述。
如果我不覺得我自己的存在，
或許我早就離開了我的肉體。

我們的生存不是僅為生活，
而且也是搜尋真理和快樂。
科學只是儀器做我們試驗，
宗教是無範圍讓我們敬慕。
真理是非常油滑而且無窮，
它捏造顯示適合我們的目標。

與我生活有不同的涵義，
我總是有實體而且脆弱，
我的行為對我的周圍有衝擊，
我的影響可以是正或是負，
我的身體柔弱我的頭腦隱瞞，
集體的，我可能是天使或是惡魔。

我如嬰兒一樣的年輕與無知，
但世界一定有能力鑄造我的行為。
我的表現依靠我的教師，
克服障礙完全是靠我自己，
我不可能為我自己的目的而移山，
最後的結果不完全靠我的努力。

我們全認為我們有一些獨特的技能，
嘗試誕生的喜悅與死亡的哀痛，
他們全是絕望的欺騙和臨時。
在永久的支配和年齡，
我們僅僅是在晚上螢火蟲的閃光，
空虛窒息了我們個人的特徵。

2009 年 1 月 5 日

638   **Life without Form**

Life without a form is metaphysical,
Existence can be flesh, spirit or soul,
Visible or invisible is a medium of illusion,
Physical and non-physical differ in features.
If I am not aware of my own being,
Perhaps I have left my body eons ago.

Our survival is not for living only,
But also searching for truth and happiness,
Science is only an instrument for us to explore,
Religion is dimensionless for us to adore.
Truth is utterly elusive and boundless.
It fabricates a manifestation to fit our goal.

Living with me has a different connotation,
I am always physical and also vulnerable.
What I do has an impact to my surrounding,
My influence can be positive or negative,
My body is meek but my mind is covert,
Collectively, I could be an angel or a devil.

I was infantile when young and naive,
But the world certainly has power to mold.
How I behave depends on my mentors,
To overcome the obstacle is up to me.
I can't move a mountain for my own purpose,
The outcome is not fully based on my effort.

We all think we have some unique skills,
Tasting the joy of birth and sorrow of death,
They are all hopelessly deceptive and temporary.
In the age and disposition of perpetuity,
We are merely a flash from a firefly at night,
Our individuality smothered by the void.

Jan. 5, 2009

645　真理有它自己的形式

您可能寫的只有那麼多，
因此作家和詩人都是海盜，
他們在這裡搶一點線索，那裡一點概念，
字就像冬天雪花一樣的便宜，
如果你有點聰明任何人都能捉一點，
然後加少量的胡椒粉及一點鹽，
靈巧的把他們打成蛋白和奶油酥。

讀小說就像遇見一個陌生人，
在幾頁或兩三個章節以後，
您可能猜測整個內情。
在瞥眼之下去判斷一個人，
經常導致準確人品。
第一個直覺觀像刀子一樣的鋒利，
我們切的不是蛋糕而是行為。

印象主要的是視之而定，
我們愛或恨一個人純粹是個人性。
判斷人的性格好壞是才能，
表面行為像一張薄紙，
它既不可能包著火和水，
確實性是有根據而不是謊言，
真理的美是有它自己的品位。

知覺是領悟的橋梁，
沒有它我們是在恍惚蒙昧。
良心是公正的城堡，
缺乏它造成我們腐壞的根基。
我們的世界不是如*蒙內*所繪，
也不是由*馬勒*交響樂來會味，
我們只是享用它而不是以它所為。

生活的藝術是永久性的休閒，
生活的幸福不等於生命的幸福，
我們沒有測量快樂的標度。
未能成名的苦惱是無益，
痛苦您沒有的財產是徒然。
我們每次使用一把牙刷去刷牙，
我們吃的只有一個腸胃去消化。

645   **Truth has its own style**

There is only so much you can write,
So writers and poets are all pirates,
They rob a notion here, a hint there,
Words are as cheap as winter snowflakes,
Anyone can catch them if you have wit,
Adding a pinch of salt and a touch of pepper,
Cleverly whip them just like a soufflé.

Reading a novel is like meeting a stranger,
After a few pages or a couple of chapters,
You may be able to guess the entire tale.
Judging a person after a quick glance,
Often leads to the accurate personality.
The first intuition is as sharp as a knife,
We are not cutting a cake but behaviors.

Impressions are largely provisional,
We love or hate a person purely personal.
A good judgment of character is a gift,
Superficiality is like a piece of thin paper,
It can neither wrap fire nor water,
Authenticity is authentic not from a lie,
The beauty of truth is in its own style.

Consciousness is a bridge to awareness,
Without it we are in a state of trance.
Conscience is the citadel to righteousness,
Lack of it leads us to the corruptive base.
Our world is not painted by Monet's brush,
Nor expressed by Mahler's symphonies,
We use it for our benefit but do not live by it.

The art of life is perpetual leisure,
Happy living is not equal to a happy life,
There is no scale to measure happiness.
Torment of not becoming famous is futile,
Anguish for what you do not own is fruitless.
We use one brush at a time to brush teeth,
And one stomach to digest what we eat.

648　早春的溶解

溫暖的早春太陽,
照過我房間的天窗,
那些柔嫩的楓樹枝,
輕微的在風中舞動及搖擺。

樹枝尚未發芽,
仍帶來幾分喚醒的蹤影,
與渴望春天的懷戀。

噢!令人愉快早春的融化,
與垂滴與啜泣的屋簷,
冰流的不是血液而是淚珠。

不要那麼冷酷與僵硬,
冬天在您的衣袖之下,
毫不關心無辜,
和在街道上徘徊的窮人。

我們應該在和諧中相互共存,
你鬆懈少許我們採納一吋,
為什麼您為喪失意志而流淚?

在永恆循環之下,
您會在一個新的季節內再生,
我們將退化進入微不足取,
或永不會恢復我們的本身。

在不可預知的時間和地點,
我們會在另一個領域相會,
有意或無意的分享撫慰。

2009 年 2 月 9 日

648   **Early Spring Thaw**

The warm early spring sun,
Shining through the skylight into my room,
Those tender branches of maple trees,
Lightly swinging and dancing in the wind.

Trees are not yet sprouting,
Still bringing a few traces of awakening,
With the nostalgia of longing for spring.

Oh! What a delightful untimely thaw,
With weeping and crying eaves,
Ice is bleeding not blood but tears.

Do not be so cold and stiff,
Winter was under your sleeve,
Cared not for the unfortunate,
And the destitute wandered in the street.

We should co-exist equally in harmony,
You give a little and we take a bit,
Why are you so unnerved shedding tears?

In the eternity of recycling,
You will be reborn in a new season,
We will be degenerated into unknown,
Perhaps never regain our identity.

In the unforeseeable time and place,
We will meet again in another dominion,
Knowingly or unknowingly share solace.

Feb. 9, 2009

649　飛蛾的精神

您不可能在湖水釣你的影子，
亦不能用網去捕捉新鮮。
我們教導善而不是惡，
在自然真實事物的本質而非偽造。
我們都像飛蛾衝擊燈火，
為我們自身利益或慾望，
只有玻璃預防我們的崩潰。

快速和滾動黑暗的雲彩，
到處減弱明亮的太陽，
在原野微弱朦朧的薄霧，
一波一浪的閃爍散發微光，
突然噪聲震驚了鳥兒們，
那是什麼？
在遠處，輕輕的叫喊。

這些都是神祇的玩弄，
他們經常給以極度的傷害，
不應該的誤引我們跟隨。
也不擔當義務或職責。
我們仍然繼續的崇拜他們，
好像海龜尋找溫暖的海灘，
期望他們像是陽光一樣的燦爛。

我們大都是在海上無先見的旅客，
當沒有太陽，星圖及星辰。
在太平洋深處的磷光條紋，
總是排列或指向最近的地帶，
提供海員們在黑暗中一種指南，
它是否是自然創作或是神的介入？
或許，自然就是神而神是自然。

2009 年 2 月 16 日

649   **The Spirit of Moths**

You cannot fish your reflection out of water,
Nor can catch freshness with a net.
We have taught good from evil,
Real things in nature from fake.
We all like moths rush to a lamp,
For our own self-interest or desire,
Only glass prevents us from demise.

The swift and rolling dark clouds,
Hither and thither wither the bright sun,
A ghostly faint mist in the meadow,
Flickers and shimmers in waves.
A sudden noise startles the birds,
What was that?
In distance, cry faintly.

These are all gods' doing to us,
They often inflict terrible suffer,
And shamefully mislead us to follow.
Without any accountability or liability,
We still go on worshiping them willingly,
As if sea turtles seek the warm beach sand,
And expect they are as brilliant as sunshine.

Most of us are visionless ocean travelers,
When there is no sun, no stars and no chart.
The phosphorescent streaks deep in Pacific,
Always aligning or pointing to the nearest land,
Providing navigators a guide in the darkness,
Is it a natural setting or the divine creation?
Perhaps, natures are gods and gods are natures.

Feb. 16, 2009

651　時間變化的塵埃

噢! 那些兇猛嗥叫狂風，
搖動門窗冷卻我的勁骨，
在此連綿不盡的漫長冬天，
為什麼您就不能饒了我們？

在一個可怕陰暗的夜晚，
我埋在一堆溫暖的駝絨被，
安慰我的神經啜飲熱茶，
來抵擋您那橫蠻的恐嚇。

我沒有十足喜歡或不喜歡，
對所有大自然的喜怒無常，
我們都非常微小與衰弱，
詛咒它們全是徒勞無功。

為了生存我必須呼吸，
也同樣的包括失望和汙染，
我吞進希望吐出幻滅，
及我們可憐情感的負重。

未來遠景好像風一樣的不確定，
過去的記憶塗上一層茫然，
現在吹走了夢想與幻影，
光陰消除感傷的灰塵。

保持我的警惕追求未知，
我總是延伸我地平線的界限，
對我那些朋友和同事，
我謹慎我的言詞和相應行動。

至於我能做或不能做，吃或是喝，
它純粹是必要而不是偶然，
您是否在節儉或奢侈的生活，
生命最後對待您將是平等。

2009 年 2 月 21 日

651   **The Dust of Changing Time**

Oh! Those ferocious howling winds,
Rattling shutters and chilling my bones,
In this endless peril of long winter,
Why can't you just leave us alone?

It is an ominous and gloomy night,
I am burying in a pile of warm quilt,
Sipping hot tea and soothing my nerve,
Fending off your unruly menace.

I have no great liking or disliking,
To all natural furies and temperaments,
We are very minuscule and feeble,
Cursing them is trivial and hardly relevant.

What I inhale is for my survival,
But also contaminants and disappointments,
I gulp in hope and exhale disillusion,
Bear burdens of my own pity emotions.

Future prospects are uncertain as the wind,
Memory was coated with a layer of abstraction,
Present blows away all dreams and illusions,
Time wipes off the dust of sentiment.

Keeping me vigilant, pursuing unknown,
I constantly push the boundary of my horizon,
To those who were friends and colleagues,
I guarded my words and acting accordingly.

As to what I do or can't do, eat or drink,
It is pure necessary and not by accident,
Whether you live in thrift or in extravagant,
Life will treat you equally in the end.

Feb. 21, 2009

653　借用了肢翼

我的耳朵充滿了噪音，
我的頭泛濫著憂慮。
我像鳥一樣的在空中飛行，
在雲上滑翔用人家的肢翼。
我看見下面黑暗和成群的光輝，
像蜘蛛網上閃爍的露珠。

一切都閃閃而過包括我的存在，
我失去了比我感傷更多的見解。
在不停的向西行動之下，
我掙得到幾小時無意義的直覺，
時間減速天日加長，
當我回頭時我將必須償還。

如此的轉移誤置了我天然的穩定，
從嚴寒到一個晴朗的地點，
天氣宜人但態度低劣，
金黃色的海灘不能消除我的暈眩。
我失去的不僅我的安詳和寧靜，
也丟掉我的休閒與殷勤。

在炎熱的環境和快速的行動，
也帶來易於激動的性情，
在鬆弛和振奮之間的矛盾。
或者在道德或責任的衝突。
我被放進苛刻與倉促生活方式，
值得信任和真誠並不很流行。

在荒野煩亂不寧的漂泊之後，
我最後回到富有情理的藏身地，
讓我的周圍來安慰無禮的傲慢。
編鐘偶然鳴響出輕鬆的音樂，
我很欣賞但不知道它的起源，
我請願是譏誚的傻瓜而不是粗俗的人。

在土壤裡勤奮的勞動之後，
我安靜的坐在我庭院裡思考，
附近路上的吵鬧好像川溪，
在河裡流動的不是水，
而是人間不停的衝擊。
我現在是一個沒有借用肢翼的人。

653 With Borrowed Wings

My ears saturated with metallic sound,
My mind flooded with apprehension.
I am flying high in the air as if a bird,
Soaring above clouds with borrowed wings.
I see darkness below with glittering clusters,
Like dew drops sparkle on the spider webs.

Everything flashes by including my existence,
I lose more perception than my sentiment.
Under the continual westward motion,
I gain a few hours of meaningless intuition,
Time slows down a bit and day lengthens,
I will have to give it all back when I return.

The shift misplaces my natural stability,
From the bitter cold to a sunny location,
Weather is pleasant but manners are rotten,
Golden beach did not smooth my qualm.
I lost not only my serenity and peace,
But also my leisure and attentiveness.

In the hot milieu and fast movement,
Coming with also the hot temperament,
Morality and liability are at variance,
Stagnancy clashes with effervescence,
I was deposited into a rushed ways of life,
Conviction and sincerity are not prevalent.

After having drifted restlessly in the wildness,
I finally returned to my refuge of senses,
Let my surroundings sooth petty insolences.
A chime is tingling with a casual tune,
I cannot distinguish its origin but enjoy it,
I prefer being a cynical fool than a vulgar man.

After a stringent cultivation with the soil,
I sit quietly meditating in my garden,
Noise from the nearby road as if streams,
What's flowing in the river is not water,
But the endless rushes of humans.
I am now the one without a borrowed wing.

655　自由詩的贖罪

在一條落寞和荒涼的路上,
遠景是我聖潔的所有。
星星在上指南我的旅途,
我認識也知道他們,
但不願他們來得更近。
在朋友之間保留一點距離是明智,
迷濛易於隱瞞可憐的缺點。

在夜深和黑暗晚間,
我夢見死亡和再生,
醒來後聽見有人的聲音。
我不知道從那裡來或是誰,
它是我自己的知覺或是離子空間?
詩詞從我的內在流出,
這不是幻覺而必須是實際。

死亡僅是狀態的傳變,
在界限之間缺乏傳遞,
它有鋒利的界線但目的不明。
葬禮怎能是個可愛的場合?
墓地的彙聚那能是歡悅事件。
快樂的詞句是有造化的修辭,
在這種會場合卻非常缺乏誠意。

流淚是內在苦惱的發泄,
笑不一定是坦率或真意。
讓文詞執行他們的高貴端莊,
去表達它們真正的意味,
不由偶然言辭損壞他們的品味,
詩歌是發泄情緒的煙囪,
煙霧卻代表喜悅及喪失信心。

我是我自己直覺感的奴隸,
思想帶著情感流暢,
這些都是生命中不顯著的事,
一個與生命具來的銳利感,
助長我象徵性的情操,
而不是取悅別人對我的觀感。

655   **Redemption for Free Verses**

On a desolately bleak road,
Prospect is all I have and holy.
Stars above guide me where to proceed,
I know them and what they are,
And do not wish them to come any near.
Keeping a distance among friends is wise,
Pitiful faults are concealed by the haziness.

In the deep and dark night,
I dreamt of death and rebirth,
Waking up to hear someone's voice.
I did not know from whom or from where,
Is it my consciousness or the fourth-state?
Doggerel lines of verses are hurtful,
It is not an illusion and it must be in reality.

Death is only the transformation of state,
And lacks transmission between boundaries,
It has a sharp edge and reason is unclear.
How can a funeral be a lovely occasion?
Or a gravesite gathering is a joyous affair?
Cheerful words are blissful rhetoric,
But lack context in the occasion.

Shedding tears releases inner distress,
Laughter is not always candid or sincere.
Let the words perform their dignities,
Conveying their true meaning of flavors,
Not by casual discourse to spoil their tastes.
Poetry is a chimney to vent sentiment,
Smoke represents despair as well as joy.

I am a slave to my own intuition,
Thoughts flow freely with emotion,
These are unremarkable things in life,
A keen sense with beget perception,
Facilitating my metaphoric sentiment,
Not pleasing someone else's idea of me.

658　搖籃

在一棵光禿的小楓樹下，
我看著四月孤獨的新月，
像小船一樣低低的在西部天空。
來自無邊，
去至無際，
啊!耐心點，我的夥伴，
她的目的地 - 天邊。

寒冷的微風，飽和的濕氣，
露珠從水淋淋的樹枝點滴，
它們嘗起來有點黏與甜。
它是來自土壤或是楓樹液？
噯呀!我知道 - 土壤，
濘泥及散沙的表兄弟，
他們與水黏合不是血液。

農夫的生命線，
蠕蟲為家，植物的母親，
我們把它塑成不同的形狀，
它總是回到自然形式的塵埃，
在過程中，我們只是它的奴隸。

他們說我是一位好耕種者，
滿菜園茂盛的綠葉，
我不是一個為贏利的地主，
只是為朋友和我自己而種植。
是在我老年的一個恭維。

2009 年 4 月 3 日

658 **Cradles**

Under a small naked maple tree,
I see the lonely crescent moon in April,
Low in the western sky like a boat,
Coming from boundless,
Going to boundless unknown,
Oh! Patience, my good man,
I know her destination – horizon.

Chilly breeze saturated with moisture,
Dewdrops drip from the dripping tree,
They taste slightly slimy and sweet.
It is from maple sap or from dirt?
Aha! I know it - soil,
Cousins of mud and sand,
They're bound by water not blood.

Peasants' livelihood,
Home for worms, mother for plants,
We mould it into different shapes,
It always returns to its dust form,
In the process, we are only its slaves.

They say I am a good farmer,
Full garden of the lush greens,
I am not a planter for gain,
Only grow for myself and friends,
A pleasure in my old age

April 3, 2009

659　混合搖籃的詩節

在棵，
小楓樹下，
我看著娥眉月，
像小船在西部天空，
孤獨。

從天涯海角，
來往未知的無限，
耐心點，夥伴，
我知道她的預定，
自自然然是天邊。

冷顫，
空氣露珠，
從滴水的樹枝，
嘗起來有點黏和甜。
泥嗎？

啊! 我知道 - 土
濘泥及散沙表兄弟，
非血液是水。

農夫生命線，
蟲之家植物之母，
我們塑各形，
它總是回到塵埃，
我們是它的奴隸。

我是耕種者，
滿菜園茂盛綠葉，
我不為贏利，
只為朋友和自己，
是我老年的樂趣。

　　搖籃混合詩，包括各種形式及音節數目，其中有，二四六八二，及 日本俳句詩 有 五七五 與 五七五七七。

659   **Stanza of Mixed cradle**

Under
A maple tree,
I see the crescent moon,
In the western sky like a boat,
Alone.

Coming from boundless,
Going to boundless unknown,
Oh! Patience, my man!
I know her destination,
Naturally - horizon.

Chilly!
Air with dewdrops,
Drip from the dripping tree,
They taste slightly slimy and sweet,
From dirt?

Oh! I know it - soil,
Cousins of mud and dry earth,
Not by blood but water.

Peasants' livelihood,
Home for worms and mother for plants,
We mould it into shapes,
It returns to its dust form,
We are only its slaves.

I am a farmer,
My garden full of lush greens,
I plant not for gain,
Only for friends and myself,
A delightful endeavor in my old age.

Stanza of mixed cradle, including the combination of different number of syllabus, the typical ones are 2 4 6 8 2, 5 7 5 and 5 7 5 7 7. Last two forms are Japanese Haiku.

660　笨拙也是才幹

我像騾子一樣的倔強和笨拙,
善於沈默但言說卑劣,
又不能保留與人有持久的關係。
我總是搬移石磚和修建橋樑,
愚蠢地的相信有些人會受益,
但他人經常損毀我的努力。

我以為我的身體會更加順從,
很快體會到我真正身體的天分,
當我失手掉下工具或翻倒油漆,
擊中我的拇指而不是釘子,
然後劇烈的詛咒我的釘錘,
而不是抨擊我的愚笨。

我寧可摸弄冷的物質,
玩弄溫暖的骨肉有它的後果,
按摩者是最幸運的人,
屠夫繼承油膩的手指。
我粗修機器及器具,
沒有外科醫生血淋淋的手指。

我拆卸機器不是骨肉,
不必掩藏我的罪行和獲利,
我製造抽象性的破爛小雕塑,
為新奇囤積居奇備件,
我憔悴的身體就像舊貨,
有時,它會變得得心應手。

我做的來自天然,
在缺乏條件和玩具中成長,
對那些同事和朋友,
我謹慎我的言詞如同是陌生人。
敵友並不互相排斥,
忠誠或可靠僅是虛構。

2009年6月8日

660   **Clumsiness is Talent**

I am clumsy and stubborn as a mule,
Good in silence but poor in voice,
Lasting relationships I can't keep.
I love moving bricks and erecting bridges,
Foolishly believing someone may benefit,
But they often gut out my best effort.

Perhaps my body may be more diligent,
Soon realizing my real bodily talent,
When I drop tools and spill paint,
Hitting my thumbnail instead of nails,
Then bitterly cursing my hammer,
Rather than slamming my clumsiness.

I prefer fiddling with cold substances,
Playing with warm flesh has its consequences.
Massagers are the most fortunate,
The butchers inherit only greasy fingers.
I tinker merely with gadgets and appliances,
Do not have bloody hand of a surgeon.

I disassemble machines not bodies,
Neither hide my crime nor for gain,
Only making abstract junk statuettes,
And hoarding spare parts for novelty,
My old body just likes my scraps,
Once in a while, they become handy.

I did what I did coming very natural,
Growing up lacking means and toys,
To those who were colleagues and friends,
I guarded my words as with strangers.
Friends and foes are not mutually exclusive,
Loyalty and trust are only a fable.

June 8, 2009

662　無足輕重

我是有形也是無形，
這個世界將持續穩步前進，
有無我卑躬的努力，
我的生存是由於我的存在，
認不認識我是毫不相關。

我一直在做我要做的事，
先爬小丘再登高山，
在我後面不遠總是充滿失敗。
為了我自己的生存而不被淹沒，
我保持抬頭和睜開雙眼。

我們都在生命中徒勞，
他們是否是無意義或可貴，
流汗是謙遜與高尚，
最重要的事也許是看不見，
為自滿努力也是值得。

我像蜜蜂或花草貢獻我的本份，
他們授粉與豐富環境，
收集蜂蜜與分散花粉。
我勞力、修補及修剪庭院，
保持健康和我心懷愉快。

我無怨言為什麼要去做，
總是少許寫作廣泛閱讀，
靜靜的哭與笑而閉嘴，
以更多的力量去擦乾眼淚，
希望明天會有點愉快與振奮。

2009年4月22日

662   No Consequences

I am visible and yet invisible,
This world will continue forging ahead,
With or without my meek effort,
I exist because of my existence,
Knowing me or not is irrelevant.

I do what I always do,
Climbing hills first then higher mountain,
The flood of failures is always not far behind.
For my own sake from drowning,
I keep my head high and eyes open.

We all do a lot of futile things in life,
Whether they are valuable or pointless,
Sweating is humble and shedding it is noble,
The most important thing may not be seen,
The self-satisfaction is worth the effort.

I contribute my share like bees or grasses,
They pollinate flowers and enrich the environment,
And collect honey and spread pollen.
I labor, tinker and manicure gardens,
Getting trim and keeping my heart warm.

I do not quarrel much for what I do,
And always write a little and read a lot,
Cry quietly and laugh with mouth shut,
I dry my tears with an additional vigor.
Hoping tomorrow will be a bit cheerful.

April 22, 2009

663　歪曲的觀察

我沉入我的靜止精神狀態，
觀看下落的月牙。
我把我的頭埋在枕頭為了保證，
月亮為新的天際私奔。
啊!您那可憐愛看天的朝聖者，
羨慕經常是片面的喜愛。

從夢的夢裡醒來，
我用我有模糊判斷的鑰匙，
打開另一天的視窗，
閘門在我的床邊洞開，
生活向前衝刺毫無頭尾，
像夢一樣的輕微像蝸牛樣的無目標。

早晨開始有精采的日出，
但我在盲目的強光中蒼白無光，
我繪製沒有生動的顏色或題材，
寫作又無激動的喜怒哀樂，
在奮鬥中連續的痛苦，
我僅是一個自作愚蠢夢想家。

我的身體啼哭全是汗水，
用眼淚洗滌我的睫毛和前額，
我的眼睛支配我去聽，
我的耳朵要我去看。
我對我看見沉溺和興奮，
是在我年齡的少數快樂。

興高采烈是在生命中瞬變開花，
淒涼棲息我們整年，
我們也許半身埋在土中，
但仍然在沙漠中繪製海市蜃樓，
和支付我們愚笨的債務，
而看不見慾望是無底洞。

2009 年 4 月 4 日

663   Skewed Observation

I am sinking into my resting frame,
Watching the setting crescent moon
I bury my head in pillows for assurance,
The moon elopes away for the new horizon.
Ah! You poor old patriotic sky pilgrim,
Admiration is often one-sided affection.

Awakening from a dream of dreams,
Using the key of my misty judgment,
Opening the doors for a new beginning,
The floodgate unlocks beside my bed,
Life thrusts ahead without head and tail,
Trivial as a dream and aimless as a snail.

Morning begins with a brilliant sunrise,
But I am colorless in the blinding glares,
I paint without idyllic colors or themes,
Writing verses without punching premise.
Continuous torment in the struggle,
I am only a self-made foolish dreamer.

My body cries with drenching sweat,
Tears wash my eyelashes and forehead,
I hear what my eyes direct me to listen,
And see where my ears want me to look.
I am indulging and joyful to what I perceive,
The few thrills I get at my age.

Euphoria is a transient blossom in life,
Desolation inhabits remained of the year.
We may be half-buried in our grave,
But still painting mirages in the desert,
And paying debts for our foolishness,
Not seeing desires is bottomless.

April 4, 2009

290　良藥

出生，
導致苦惱和疼痛，
母親要比嬰兒多，
到時候，
痛總是會趕上你，
首先是擦傷膝蓋，
和割傷指頭，
失去的糖果或未能拿到你的禮物。

成年的痛苦都是自作，
煩惱好的工作，
與適當的職業，
為了光榮、出名與富有，
與朋友和婚姻之間的交戰，
精神上的健忘，
與身體上的疲倦。

光陰及年齡沒有仁慈，
不定性的頭痛和胃潰瘍，
風濕性的紅腫或骨關節炎，
老人癡呆也許會免除你的苦惱，
卻導致你家庭的負擔，
與困苦。

我們傾家蕩產來治病，
整修骨折治療四肢，
復原我們惡化的身體，
也許死亡是世界上的良藥，
消除創傷及終止痛苦。

2005年六月三十日

　　我們花費大量資金設法治療疾病，在最後仍然逃脫不了死亡，或許死是最佳的良藥去消除痛苦和創傷。

290   Best Medicine

Birth,
Inducing agony and pain,
More so to mothers than infant,
In time,
The pain will catch up with you,
First cut on fingers,
And scrape on knees,
Candies you lost or gifts you didn't receive.

Pains are self made in our prime age,
Wrestling for good jobs,
And right professions,
For glory, for riches and for fame,
Battle between friends and marriage,
Suffer for mental amnesia
and physical fatigue.

Time and age are kindless,
Migrant headache and stomach ulcer,
Osteoarthritis or rheumatoid inflammation,
Alzheimer may free you from agony,
But induce hardship
and burden to your family.

We spend fortune to cure diseases,
Repair broken bones and mend joints,
Rehabilitating our deteriorated body,
Perhaps death is the perfect medicine,
End suffering and erase pain.

June 30, 2005

We spend fortune finding ways to cure diseases, in the end still could not escape death. Perhaps death is the best medicine to erase pain and suffering.

667　一陣風

我聽見雷聲在遙遠的地方，
閃電打開黑暗的眼睛，
雨珠梳刷過骯髒的空氣，
點點、滴滴、濺潑及噴散，
我無目的與茫然計數，
然後像冬眠的熊沉沉的入睡。

我們不可能登天，
亦不可能接近地核，
世上只有少數者達成偉大，
我們甚而沒有那些妄想，
我不屬於那兩者之一，
叫狼來了又有何益。

我們彙聚有如一陣微風，
短暫的好像閃電，
遙遠的猶如雷雨，
近的像似雨聲。
我們是否再能見面，
與下場風雨無關。

我通常是在照像機的後面，
並不經常看我自己的背影，
用棍子與我的家犬走路，
手杖不是支撐我的步伐，
家犬也未引導我的方向，
然而，我像豬搽口紅的一樣。

我不應該坐在這裡吠叫，
追我自己的尾巴也是無益，
或者叫罵褻瀆然後感到抱歉。
以往看起來總是甜美，
期待將來都是有期望，
只有目前才是不堪設想。

2009 年 5 月 17 日

667   **Passing Gale**

I hear thunder in the distance,
Lightning opens the eyes of darkness,
Raindrops comb through grimy air,
Drip, drop, splatter and spatter,
I count them blindly and aimlessly,
And then fall sound asleep like a bear.

We cannot reach the pinnacle of sky,
Nor capable touching the core of earth,
There are only a few achieving greatness,
We do not even have the imagination.
I belong to neither of those collections,
And crying wolf in itself is pointless.

We gather here likes the passing gale,
Brief as if the lightning flashes,
Remote as the distant thunder,
And close as the sound of the rain.
Whether we will meet again,
The coming storm is irrelevant.

I was usually behind the camera,
And did not see the image of my back,
Walking my dog with a stick,
The cane did not support my steps,
Dog did not guide my direction,
Yet, I am like a pig wearing lipstick.

I should not sit here barking,
Fruitlessly chasing my own tail,
Or screaming profanity then feeling sorry.
Looking back in the past is sweet,
Hope for the future is hopeful,
Only the present is hopeless.

May 17, 2009

668 禪教信徒的特色

我們都有容貌與面貌,
有些人比其他人出名,
臭名昭彰製造醜名遠揚,
高貴的行為不須要高尚。
我們的出現像似圖像,
僅僅是血肉平面的投射,
歪曲的心地總是埋沒無形。

身體的感觸是膚膜的意識,
溫暖的肉體摸起來很享受,
為了滿足我們的慾望,
為了縱情放蕩與風采,
我們尋找我們缺乏的東西,
不是為我們生存而是縱容,
埋在皮膚之下的仍然是掩藏。

禪教信徒尋求內在的啟示,
不帶行李及負擔去旅行,
一種信條主要是探索放棄。
精神病醫生探索心胸的黑暗,
手指微弱的抽動也是異常,
正常行動在他們的察視也是反常,
神志清楚取決以誰的測量。

我們出生全時是無辜,
然後繼承仇恨及傲慢,
財富和勢力製造偏見,
貧窮引起我們心靈不安,
幻滅促使人群更加惱怒,
憤世嫉俗導致擺脫幻想,
我們的行為反應我們的教養。

2009 年 5 月 26 日

668   Zenist's Traits

We all have a visage,
Some are more known than others,
Notorious behaviors create notoriety,
Noble deeds need no nobility.
Our appearance is in the form of image,
Merely flat projection of a bloody body,
Gnarled and wrinkled heart is buried.

Body sensation is the sense of membrane,
Warm flesh is pleasure for touch,
For the sake of satisfying our desire,
For the love of orgy and style,
We are seeking things we are lacking,
Not for our own survival but indulgence,
What's buried under the skin is still hidden.

Zenists search the internal enlightenment,
Traveling without luggage and burden,
A doctrine quests largely the abandonment.
Psychiatrists explore the darkness of mind,
A small twitch of fingers is anomalous,
A normal action is abnormal in their scrutiny.
Sanity depends on whose measurement.

We were born with an innocent mind,
Then inherit hatred and arrogance,
Wealth and power create prejudice,
Poverty turns us into uneasiness,
Disillusion drives crowd angrier,
Cynicism generates disenchantment,
Our behaviors reflect our upbringing.

May 26, 2009

669　預期命運的歌曲

我聽見有人在我耳邊唱歌*：
在一個預先決定年月的一天，
您在空虛中的空虛，
在夢中編織的一場夢，
您的面孔蒼白的像一片枯葉，
說再見並不需要，
為什麼不就安靜的離去?

我醒過來回想我所聽見的，
我看不見悲傷或哭臉，
也沒有放棄或寂寞。
來去並不重要，
在死亡預感中的寧靜場景，
沒有疾病和病痛的延伸，
也許是一個崇高的境遇。

沒有人問候和說再見，
空氣似乎從空間吸盡，
情緒沉重如水泥，
強制的笑臉有一種空虛的感覺。
我知道許多的送行沒有情感，
少許的別離甚而慶興;
此次分離卻有一種鬼祟的感觸。

那裡還有一個最後的告別，
沒有誇耀和選擇，
我們要走的路乃是孤獨旅行，
沒有護送及伴侶，
唯一的指燈是螢火蟲，
我們的相遇只能在夢中。

站在一條小路的末端，
在城市的一個街角，
在高原或在傾斜小山邊，
看著地平線慢慢的消失，
平靜的安祥的面對去路，
我去了一個附近的領域，
不是骨肉而是心靈。

*從一首中國歌翻譯來的大意

669   A Song of Pre-destiny

I hear someone's singing in my ear: *
One day in a predestined year,
You are in the void within the void,
Weaving dreams within a dream,
Your face is pale like a withered leaf,
Why not just calmly come and quietly leave,
Saying goodbye is not needed.

I retraced what I had heard,
And saw no sad or crying face,
There was no abandonment or loneliness,
Coming or going has no significance,
A premonition of death in a serene scene,
Without prolonging sickness and disease,
Perhaps it's a noble predicament.

No one said hello or goodbye,
The air seems sucked out from space,
Sentiment is as heavy as cement,
Forced smile has a sense of emptiness.
I knew many sending offs without emotion,
A few going away even with elation;
This departure has a feeling of stealth.

There is always a final farewell,
Once for a lifetime for everyone,
Without fanfare or alternative,
The road one has to travel is lonely,
No escort and no companion,
The guiding lights are fireflies,
The only meeting place is in a dream.

Standing at one end of a small road,
At the street corners of a city,
On a plateau or on a sloped hill,
Watching horizons slowly disappear,
Quietly and peacefully facing the outcome,
I went to a nearby domain,
Not in flesh but in spirit.

* Loosely translated and from a Chinese song.

671　裸露的隱喻

晚間的曙光慢慢退色，
桃紅色的地平線變灰，
光亮沈默的從我們這裡撤走，
直到它不留下一點微弱的蹤跡，
我試著抓住它的鬍鬚，
黑暗卻吞咽它整個尾巴。

我張開我的眼睛越來越寬，
看見僅是被侵蝕的黑暗，
我抽回我困乏的眼力，
延伸我感官的觸角，
觸摸、傾聽、感受或嗅覺，
大氣空洞的就像似死亡。

我然後體會到是多麼愚蠢，
看見就相信在這裡不適用，
空氣及水蒸氣包圍著我們，
輻射彌漫著整個空間，
電磁波泛濫我們骨肉，
沒有黑暗，光輝就失去它的壯麗。

突然，綠色的閃光，
啊! 螢火蟲，
一隻微小的昆蟲，我的武士，
閃光不是為了照明，
而是照亮您的不安及心靈，
我們經常說光亮在搖撼，
但不承認我們自己的不穩定。

我擁有整個的視野。
仍然認為世界拋棄了我，
光總是擁抱了所有的我們，
黑暗不忽略任何人，
它是在我們眼睛裡不是在我們機智，
空虛僅是赤裸的象徵。

2009 年 6 月 6 日

671 Naked Metaphor

Evening twilight fades slowly,
Red and pink horizon turns to gray,
Light silently withdraws from us,
Until it leaves not even a faint trace,
I try to hold its whiskers,
The darkness swallows its entire tail.

I open my eyes wider and wider,
Seeing only the encroached darkness,
Pulling back my wary eyesight,
Extending the horns of my senses,
Touch, listen, feel and smell,
The air is empty as death.

Realizing then what a fool I am,
Seeing is belief does not apply here,
Air particles and water vapor surround us,
Radiation permeates the entire space,
Electromagnetic waves flood our bones,
Without darkness, light loses its glory.

Suddenly, a flash of green light,
Oh! A firefly,
A tiny insect, my knight,
The flashes are not for illumination,
But lighten your discomfort and spirit,
We often say that the light is shaking,
But not admitting we are unsteady.

I have the entire view to myself,
Still thinking the world has deserted me,
Light has always embraced us,
Darkness does not neglect anyone,
It is in our eyes, not in our wit,
Emptiness is only naked metaphor.

June 6, 2009

673　時間流逝的走廊

他們坐在黑陰暗的角落,
皺紋的皮膚和蒼白的臉,
垂頭在他們的胸前,
不整潔睡衣雜亂頭髮,
不期待任何事件出現,
訪客經過他們的沒有一瞥,
世界輕率的把他們拋棄。

他們曾經全都是年輕充滿活力,
英俊、有吸引力、性感和精力充沛,
他們的身體洋溢誘惑的氣味,
不可抗拒的肌膚和動彈的乳房,
在他們有生命力的高峰,
她們的姿態吸引您的羨慕,
您在她們招致之下全被迷惑。

連接那些個體是非常困難,
沒有深刻的厚道及愛慕,
徹底審查他們的過去和現在,
唯一的真實是經過時間走廊,
我們也是在同個運行的通道,
也不會從它嚴酷的現實避免,
而我們在這裡玩弄字詞塑造智慧。

我們學到了我們希望的所學,
但沒有課程教導如何應付死亡。
在您我之間及所有生命之外,
我們分享空氣、地球與太陽,
在人生之中只有一生一死,
您死的是否光彩或是謙卑,
在那之後您再也不會面對。

老的含義是讓你獨單,
從家庭、朋友和年輕人,
一個喜新厭舊社會狠毒的循環,
也許他們把持他們的幻覺,
或者害怕看他們狼狽的未來,
把頭埋在沙子裡的駝鳥,
並不能防止命運指揮的手臂。

673 The Corridor of Time

They are sitting in the dim corners,
With wrinkled skin and pale faces,
Heads hanging above their bosoms,
With untidy pajamas and hair,
Waiting for no occurrence,
Visitors passing by them without a glance,
The world is abandoning them senselessly.

They were all young and vibrant once,
Attractive, handsome, sexy and energetic,
Their bodies permeated with scent of seduction,
With irresistible flesh and pulsating breasts,
At the prime of their life and vitality,
Their postures drew your admiration,
You were bewitched under their charm.

It is difficult connecting those entities,
Without deep kindness and affection,
Examining carefully their past and present,
The only truth is the corridor of time,
We are all in the same moving passage,
Not immune from its harsh reality,
Here we are playing words and shaping wit.

We have learned all we wished to learn,
But no lesson taught us about dying.
Beyond you, me and all living things,
We are sharing the same air, earth and sun,
There is only one death in one lifetime,
Whether you die gloriously or humbly,
After that you will never die again.

The meaning of old is being left alone,
From families, friends and by the young,
A vicious cycle of a disposing society,
Perhaps they are holding on to their illusion,
Or frightened to see their future quandary,
Burying head in sand like an ostrich,
Does not prevent the moving-hand of destiny.

674　自然的竊賊

我看見毛毛雨的頭髮，
陽光的光暈被面紗覆蓋，
薄霧及濕氣淹沒者空氣，
您可以穿它或用刀劍去砍，
哺乳動物發愁而植物興奮，
我既不咒天也不全慶祝。

日光悲哀的退出，
在陰暗天空裡躲避，
把一切籠罩在它的符咒之下，
貓頭鷹不叫，啄木鳥不啄，
蜘蛛不在雨中編織，
但是蠕蟲在我的庭院裡卻是欣喜若狂。

我聽見唱歌或哭泣的聲音，
但我看不見他們的面孔，
或者他們也許沒有臉面。
唯一的訪客是滴水、滴水及滴水，
您必須要去找您自己的賓客，
熱容量像死亡一樣的微軟。

自然的賊竊取了我們的生命力，
我們赤裸而無防衛，
它沒有羞辱，如果它有羞辱，
辨明事實如果它有事實。
帶著整袋的陰鬱，
我們的遠景是愚鈍和落寞。

昨天悄悄的滑過，
今天又重覆它的蕭條，
預言輝煌的明天只是謬妄。
他們說，年齡是富有耐力及智慧，
沒有人會要問我們任何見解，
期待它就像在沙漠等著下雨。

2009 年 6 月 21 日

674   **Thieves of Nature**

I see hairs of drizzle and rain,
The halo of sunshine shrouded in veil,
Mist and moisture inundate the air,
You can wear it or cut it with a blade,
Mammals dread and plants thrill,
I neither curse the sky nor celebrate.

Daylight sorrowfully bowed out,
Hidden in the glooms of the day,
Casting everything under its spell,
No owls wooing, woodpeckers pecking,
Or spiders weaving in the rain,
But worms in my garden are ecstatic.

I hear sounds of either singing or crying,
But I cannot see their faces,
Or they might not even have faces.
The only visitor is drip, drip and drip,
You will have to find your own guest,
The entropy is minuscule as death.

The thief of nature steals our vitality,
We are naked and defenseless,
It has no shame if there is shame,
Discerning facts if there are facts.
With the whole sack of dreariness,
Our prospect is dull and desolate.

Yesterday voicelessly slipped by,
Today is the repeating of its cheerlessness,
Predicting bright tomorrow is fallacy.
They say, age is for endurance and wisdom,
No one cares to ask us for any opinion,
Expecting it is like waiting rain in desert.

June 21, 2009

675　相對性

光與影之間不可分,
就像在鏡子中的反映,
他們完全不同但相互依賴。
山是湖泊的相反,
流水創建小溪與河流。
買家和賣家可以互換,
但永遠不會是愛與恨。

回憶如鬼一樣難以捉摸,
它們又如你的影子的密切,
靜靜的入侵你無抵抗的世界,
一旦記憶的大門開啟,
你幾乎難能阻止其暢流,
除非你一點也不記得,
腦海裡是空白如果你不曉得。

從現在到未來之間或其後,
他們必真的像光的照明,
但您不能擁有或觸摸他們。
在比喻中從一岸到另一岸,
那裡總是有一線相連,
虹橋僅是一種幻覺,
它只是存在雨後或日落之前。

沒有藍天白雲是多麼枯燥,
沒有顏色花就失去它們的色彩。
男性與女性有天然的差異,
大肚子的男子並不缺少吸引力,
平坦胸乳可能健康但不性感,
頭變光禿心地不善,
智慧不是年齡的開花。

我們每一天穿脫衣衫,
擁抱黎明拋去黃昏,
脫落了數百萬死皮膚細胞,
增長年歲失掉節操。
我們每刻都在變更,
新陳代謝不停的摧毀與創造,
人生是由生命才導致死亡。

675   Counterpart

Light and shadow are inseparable,
Like a reflection of an object in the mirror,
They are unlike but mutually dependable.
Mountains and lakes are in the reverse,
Flowing water creates streams and rivers.
Buyers and sellers are interchangeable.
But never in the love and hate scenario.

Memories are elusive as ghosts,
They are as genuine as your shadow,
Silently invade your passive world,
Once the gate of memory is unlocked,
You can hardly stop its flow, except,
Nothing flows if you don't remember,
The reservoir is bare if you don't know.

Between now and then or thereafter,
They are real as the illumination of light,
But you can never hold or touch them.
From one bank to another in metaphor,
There is always a stretch of connection,
The bridge of rainbow is merely an illusion,
It exists mostly after rain before sunset.

Clouds would be dull without blue sky,
Flowers lose their delicacy without color.
Male and female have natural differences,
Bulged belly man implies not less attractive,
Flat chest may be healthy but no sex appeal,
Head becoming bald but mental hairy,
Wisdom is not the blossom of age.

We dress and undress each day,
Embracing dawn then casting off dusk,
Shedding off millions of dead skin cells,
Growing older and losing virtue.
We are never the same in any instant,
Metabolism is creating and destroying,
It is the living that leads to death.

678 縱情前奏曲

我看到早晨天亮的蒼白，
是那麼不尋常和疏遠，
但是在沒有多久之前，
曙光是一天歡迎的時間，
在安第斯山遙遠的山頂，
極度疲勞的工作了整晚，
黎明使人振奮的光景，
我在日出後入睡，別人開始苦力。

我很自願的在它掌握下掙扎，
留心的觀察無名恆星，
我試想能讓它們有名，
亦使我自己稍有資源，
那是我以前生命的竭力，
長久之前有如那些山的遙遠，
退休後剪去我的翅翼，
笨重的金屬由筆而代替。

我並不很明智或超然，
床支撐我的身體和四肢，
毯子保持我溫暖和舒適。
一分錢乃是一分錢富有或貧寒，
胃不知道我的口袋裡有或是無。
詩人都是那麼可憐浪漫的唯心論者，
詩詞的用語創造不是真實的世界。

星在天空仍然充滿活力，
草在原野裡輕輕揮舞，
我無能為力的夾在兩者之間，
星球是如此的遙遠又無法接近，
我不得不依賴我力所能及，
野草在大草原裡非常熟悉，
多的像似夜空裡的恒星，
平凡的有如常人。

678   **Overtures of my Indulgence**

I saw pale light of the daybreak,
So unusual and alien in one morning,
But it was not so long ago,
Twilights of the day were so welcome.
After gruelingly working all night,
On the remote mountain of Andes,
It was the cheerful sight of the dawn,
I sleep after sunrise, others begin to toil.

I struggled gladly in its grip,
Attentively watching the nameless stars,
I tried to make them well known,
And also make me a bit affluent.
That was my previous life of endeavor,
Eons ago and distant as those mountains,
I clipped my wings in retirement,
Replacing heavy metal with writing pen.

I am far from wise or metaphysical,
The bed supports my limbs and body,
And blankets keep me snug and warm.
A penny is a penny for rich or for poor,
Stomach knows nothing about my pocket.
Poets are such poor romantic idealists,
The real world created not by poetic dialect.

Stars are still vibrant in the sky,
Grasses wave softly in the wilderness,
I wedged in between with moderate means,
Stars are inaccessible and remote,
I will have to rely upon what I can hold,
Grasses in the prairie are familiar,
Numerous as stars in the night sky,
Ordinary likes all the common men.

日常通勤的來往已被遺忘，
也不去注意工作場所的勾心鬥角，
我有個屋頂在我頭上及舒適的房間，
既沒有神聖的宣誓也沒有受陷。
這就是生活還是忽略的生命？
或者是戰鬥疲勞之後的享受？
您必須犧牲名譽聲望，
去換取自由與休閒。

我批載晚露和早霧，
沐浴在早晨的陽光，
手拿一杯咖啡走進花園，
晚餐後啜茶及看夕陽。
我毫無名聲但是我自己的主宰，
付了我做地球的公民的義務，
現在離開折磨和混亂，
來索取我所付出的忠心。

2009 年 7 月 4 日

The daily ritual of commuting is forgotten,
Nor mindful workplaces' under current,
I have a cozy room and a roof over my head,
Free from sacrament and entrapments.
Is this the life of living or neglecting?
Or the after battle fatigues of enjoyment?
You will have to sacrifice prestige,
Trade in for leisure and freedom.

I wear the evening dew and morning mist,
And bathe in the morning sunshine,
Walking into garden with a cup of coffee,
Sipping tea after dinner watching sunset.
I am no body yet somebody of my own,
Paid my dues as a citizen of the earth,
Now leaving the torment and chaos behind,
I am claiming the reward of my allegiance.

July 4, 2009

698　秋葉

南瓜、蜜蜂、秋葉，
它們都有一個未來，
及它們連續的存在，
生鏽的菜園柵欄與我，
漸漸的消失，
永遠沉默。

我可能做什麼呢？
耕種一小塊土地，
用我微弱的能力排列言詞，
風重新排列它們，
雨洗掉它們的存在，
長久以後，依然沉默無言。

我站在視窗的前面，
看著我不斷惡化的身影，
反射在玻璃窗，
季節變換，
落葉下降，
平靜的沉默。

2009 年 10 月 5 日

698 **Autumn Leaves**

Autumn leaves, pumpkins and bees,
They have a future,
For their continuous revitalization,
My rusty garden fence and me,
Slowly fade away,
Forever silence.

What could I be?
Cultivating a small plot of land,
Arranging words with my modest ability,
Wind rearranges them,
Rain washes away their presences,
Generations later, still silence.

I stand in front of a window,
Watching my deteriorating frame,
Reflected on the window pane,
The changing season,
And falling leaves,
Calmly silent.

Oct. 5, 2009

681　你的還是我的

所有的日子都去了哪裡？
現在又是一個月的月底。
是否陰雨沖走了它們？
或者我對時光只是漠不關心。
我坐在我窩的通常角落，
在天窗的附近面對著監視器，
這是我私人而不是公共領域，
我只聽見雨點的打擊。

一張缺乏社交動態的景色，
沒有人看見我，我也看不見別人，
但是我被書及音樂所包圍，
熱血在我的血管裡流暢。
在這裡有許多孔縫和玻璃窗，
但幾乎沒有任何陽光。
我創造我自己想像的火花，
詩句像煙花一樣的出現。

我有一個合情理的頭腦和良心。
它們仍然有功能和理性，
我們都喜歡甜蜜的搖籃曲，
但它們大部分是童話或謊言。
我已經不在數夜空的星，
天上的事件不再使我動心，
蒼天仍然是寬闊與邀請，
視窗大開，但它不再是我的模範。

我認為我有驅動力，
給世界和社會的轉動，
世界不停的向前把我留後。
在前與在後取決於誰的基準，
你的還是我的各有所異！

　　我在2007年耶魯大學慶祝杜麗哈夫萊女士所舉辦百年天文研討會中演講論文後所朗誦兩節小詩。她不幸在我們舉行午餐慶祝她真正生日那天的一周後去世。

681   **Yours or Mine**

Where have all the days gone?
It is another end of the end of month.
Did drizzle or rain wash them away?
Or I am just indifferent in its stance.
I sit in my usual corner of my nest,
Facing my monitor and nearby skylight,
This is my private not public domain,
I hear only knocking of the rain.

A picture of poor community dynamic,
Nobody sees me and I see no one,
But surrounded by my books and music,
Hot blood flows through my veins.
Here are openings and glass panes,
But there is hardly any sunlight.
I create sparkles of my own thinking,
Verses rush out like fireworks.

I have a sensible head and conscience.
They are still rational and functioning,
We are all fond of sweet lullabies,
But they are mostly fairytales or lies.
I stop counting stars in the night sky,
Heavenly events no longer give me hypes,
The sky still remains wide and inviting,
Windows wide open, but it is not my type.

I thought I was the driving force,
For the turning world and society,
The world forges ahead and leaves me behind.
Ahead or behind depends whose reference,
Yours or mine!

I recited the last two stanzas in 2007, in the Centennial Astronomical Symposium of Yale University, in celebrating Miss Dorrit Hoffleit's 100th birthday. She passed away one week later after we held a luncheon in celebrating her birthday.

682　心靈的通道

回去我年青的通道是記憶，
憂鬱及懷舊是苦與甜。
我的渴望不是奇妙的經驗，
也不是令人興奮有玩具的童年，
無保護人、陪伴或幫助者。
一個貧窮鄉村男孩只有新鮮空氣，
外國人就像機器一樣的稀奇。

不過，我總是與自然，
草原、田園、花草和樹木在一齊，
玩的是青蛙、水百合花和爛泥，
池塘游泳採取白睡蓮，
吃甜蜜多汁的桑果，
抓破膝蓋擦傷手指，
一個淘氣的男孩染著紫紅色的嘴。

我在水牛背上面亂跑周圍，
手上拿著故事書頭腦胡思亂想，
我知道在哪裡轉彎，左或是右，
上下山坡追求好奇，
碰上機會就會直追，
我注定不是一個農村的農夫，
一個不受拘束的男孩好盤根究底。

我們吃新鮮蔬菜和玉米粥，
米飯與麵條是奢侈品，
天黑之後每人就進入深深大睡，
沒有失眠、夜遊或安眠藥，
我們夢想的不是錢，
而是綠色的水稻及金黃色麥田，
和另一個豐收的心願。

一個有洪水氾濫貧窮的地區，
富裕家庭送他們的兒子去做生意，
貧困的人家賣他們女兒去做侍女。
如果你事業成功父母驕傲，
失敗者在外地就做孤魂野鬼。
我並不符合那些類別，
結果仍是一個自由精神的放牛兒。

682   Gateway of Spirit

The gateway to my youth is memory,
Melancholy and nostalgia are bittersweet.
It's not the fancy experience I am longing,
Nor an exciting childhood with toys,
I had no protector, chaperone or aid.
A country boy with fresh air nothing else,
Foreigner was as rare as machinery.

I was with nature, nevertheless,
Pastures, fields, flowers and trees,
Playing with frogs, water lilies and mud,
Swimming in pond fetching for lotus,
Eating juicy fruits of mulberries,
With bruised fingers and scratched knees,
A nutty lad with lavender tainted lips.

I roamed around on the back of a buffalo,
A storybook in hand and dreams in head,
I knew where to turn, right or left,
Up and down hills pursuing curiosities,
Walking straight to the knocks of opportunity,
I was destined not to be a rural farmer,
An unruly boy with abundant inquisitiveness.

We ate fresh vegetables and corn porridge,
Rice and noodles are luxuries,
Everyone fell sound asleep after dark,
No insomnia, sleepwalking or Ambien pill,
We dreamt not the color of green,
But golden crops and green rice paddies,
And longing for another bumper harvest.

A region in poverty with annual floods,
Wealthy families sent their sons to trade,
Poor folk sold their daughters to be maids,
Parents were proud if you succeeded in business,
Failures would die lonely on a foreign soil.
I did not fit into those categories,
A buffalo-boy ended up with a free spirit.

683　不認輸

不想被可發明的忽視,
由於需要我去製造小工具,
在幾千平方呎的屋頂上工作,
吊七十捆屋面瓦上屋頂,
老骨頭和和缺乏靈活性,
肩膀搬運和爬梯子,
我已經是無能為力。

屋頂不很高，只有 20 英尺,
對一些弱膝蓋的老年人足以夠高。
採購一台升降機成本上數千,
租用它我又無卡車載運,
要不是就聘用專業人員,
或者就是使用一點技巧和創意,
用回收材料製造一架提昇機。

我是一個有實際應用的人,
有儲存舊機械的壞習慣,
零件、輪子、杠杆、管子及滑輪,
設計與組裝只是一點小技能。
用螺釘和膠合板構造托盤,
兩個金屬管各包棍棒在內有如滑輪,
加上潤滑油助長移動性。

托盤附加支撐在梯子上滑動,
一條繩子綁在託盤經過滑輪,
一個人在梯子上頭拉,
一位在地面裝載材料,
手拉托盤而不是電動,
單調，乏味但卻有功能,
我們順利的解除所有屋面瓦。

欣賞我計劃的小工具之後,
我感到非常安慰和滿意,
合情理的人做實用的事,
因此我們克服風雨的威脅。
成捆的瓦屋面現在屋頂上,
在我的口袋裡也節省了一畢,
流了大量汗水及一點憂慮。

683   Not to be outdone

Not to be left out on the inventive,
I build gadgets out of need.
Working on a roof thousands of square-feet,
Seventy bundles of roof shingles to be lifted,
With old bones and lack of agility,
Carrying them on shoulders,
And climbing ladder is beyond my ability.

The roof is not very high, 20 feet,
But too high for old folks with weak knees,
Purchasing a ladder-lifter costs thousands,
Renting it is still too difficult to ship,
The option is hiring professionals,
Or just using a bit scheme and ingenuity,
Build a lifter with recycling materials.

I am a man with practical applications,
A bad habit of keeping old machineries,
Spare parts, wheels, rods, pipes and pulleys,
Design and assemble need of just a bit skill.
A table constructed with screws and plywood,
Two metal pipes encase two rods as wheels,
Lubricating with grease for mobility.

The cart slides on a ladder have side braces,
A rope fasten to the carriage via a pulley,
One person sits on the top of the ladder,
One loads shingles at bottom onto the table,
Pulling it by hands without electric hoister,
Straining, tedious yet functional,
We lifted all the shingles without a hitch.

Sitting back to enjoy my project and gadget,
I feel immensely satisfied and relieved,
For a sensible man does a practical thing,
We have beaten the threat of coming rain.
Bundles of shingles are now on top of roof,
A bundle of savings in the bottom of my pocket,
Shedding a lot of sweat and bit uneasiness.

687　不穩的步伐

我在考驗我的耐力，
在屋頂上輕輕的行走，
我知道我膝蓋的強弱，
和我有限制的靈巧，
錯了一步將決定我的命運。
確定與不確定難以捉摸，
我深深知道我不穩的狀態。

清晨露水和明亮的光線，
春天開花冬天白雪，
白雛菊和紫色糯鬥菜，
紅色芙蓉和黃色黑眼蘇珊，
葡萄像*耳環*，在藤子上搖擺，
蝴蝶、蒲公英子飄揚，
這像我們手掌一樣的真實。

我看見像星系一樣的白雲，
對應浩瀚空虛的藍天，
翡翠的樹葉做背景，
圍繞著彩色植物，
如果你只要稍候一會，
葉子將會枯萎，雲的形狀更改，
我們的激動與情緒並非吉祥。

我們推測什麼可能會發生，
其餘的屬於不確定性。
運氣、機會與環境，
僅是進展的工具，
確定我們的行為或遲怠。
世界不斷的向前推動，
我們好像時間運行齒輪上的斑點。

或然率將會作一切的操縱，
我們只是象棋遊戲中的棋子。
在我們表現中一件事是確定，
我們知道我們自己和我們是誰，
我們在何處和來自哪裡，
寫我們自己心愛的題材，
但未來有如我們的步伐不確定。

687   **Uncertain Steps**

I am on a mission in endurance,
Walking lightly on the roof with soft steps,
Knowing the strength of my knees,
And the limit of my dexterity,
One wrong step will determine my fate.
Certainty from uncertainty is elusive,
I am keenly aware of my shaky state.

Morning dew and bright sunshine,
Flowers in spring and winter snow white,
White daisies and purple columbines,
Red hibiscus and yellow black eyed Susan,
Grapes, *like earrings*, dangle from the vines,
Butterflies and dandelion seeds fluttering by,
These are real as the palm of our hands.

I see white spiraling clouds like galaxies,
Against the vast void blue sky,
Emerald leaves of trees in the background,
Surrounded by colorful plants,
If you wait just a little while longer,
Leaves will wilt and shape of clouds change,
Our mood and emotion are not benign.

We anticipate what might occur,
The rest belongs to uncertainty.
Luck, opportunity and circumstance,
Only the instruments of progression,
Determining how we behave or idle.
The world is continually moving forward,
We like specks moving with the wheel of time.

Probability will manipulate its muscle,
We are merely pawns in the game of chess.
One thing is certain in our manifestation,
We know ourselves and who we are,
Where we are and come from,
And writing things dear to our heart,
But future is as uncertain as our steps.

688　不是巧合

我是一個知識的收集人,
使用雨水的經理,
和一個對戶外及自然讚美者,
我以深厚的愛慕呼吸新鮮空氣,
我們既不能買又不能賣空氣。

我平均分配我的時間,
去閱讀和寫作詩篇,
在空中捕獲音樂的電波,
修東補西,發明和修理,
我的享受是自由沒有妨礙。

我不必用欠債來顯示我的富有,
也不偷竊或盜用任何人。
財富不是你擁有多少資產,
而是在您美德的滿意,
有什麼能比清靜的頭腦更昂貴?

經過長而棘手的一天之後,
我覺得精疲力竭與耗盡。
躺在床上復原療養的時候,
突然深入一會兒暈眩,
經驗一場短夢或死亡的預感。

我脫離我的身體飛進空間,
觀測下面招搖撞騙的世界,
及我自己可憐躺平的身軀。
我在現實中可以看到所有一切,
離開身體來看真是浪費精力。

我撫摸我的頭和收回我的尾巴,
我未做完的工作仍然是未完成,
沒有人會注意或關懷。
我的幸運或不幸是屬於我自己,
我不乞求任何人負擔我的攜帶。

2009 年 9 月 21 日

688　Not a Coincidence

I am a collector of knowledge,
A rainwater-usage manager,
And a admirer of nature and the outdoors,
I breathe fresh air with a heavy affection,
We can neither buy nor sell air,

I distribute my time equally,
To my readings and writing of poetry,
Capture waves of music in the air,
Tinkering around, invent and repair,
My luxury is freedom without hinder.

I do not go into debt to show I am rich,
Nor steal or embezzle from anyone.
Wealth is not what you own in assets,
But the contentment in your virtue,
What else is dear than a pristine head.

After a long and frantic day,
I felt deadly exhausted and expended.
While lying in bed recuperating,
Suddenly sinking into a moment of daze,
Having a dream of premonition of death.

I left my body fluttering into space,
Observing the mooch-hooch world below,
And my own pitiful frame stretched flat.
I could see all these in the reality,
Leaving my body to do it is wasting sweat.

I massage my head and tuck in my tail,
Things I left undone will be undone,
No one ever notices them or cares.
My fortune or misfortune is my own,
I beg no one to burden with what I carry.

Sept. 21, 2009

689　不適時代的激動

九月午夜的滿月，
金色燦爛，白光明照，
這是秋天收割的季節，
和慶祝中秋節的時間，
在農曆閏年的五月，
使我弄錯了三十天。

製造日曆的人是明智或魯莽？
來欺騙愚蠢人的激動。
我是一位頭腦簡單的人，
比較喜歡朱利安數天日曆，
由中午到中午，不是午夜到午夜，
沒有星期、年、月及紀元。

在每年秋天的季節，
天氣溫和莊稼幾乎收割，
在月光下進食月餅，
與愛人相對密談是如此浪漫。
舊的習慣只是給我幻想，
我真希望我不是那樣容易上當。

我們都會在節日有點懷舊，
抬頭賞明月，
低頭思想你的家園和失去青春，
我們在各地看到同樣的月亮，
但對每位卻有不同的感傷，
不是每個人都喜歡月光。

我在尋索值得高興的事，
拋棄不值得哭的感慨，
凝視著大陸與海洋，
看著升降的太陽，
我渴望寧靜與知足，
月光只是帶給我心情沮喪。

2009 年 9 月 6 日中秋節

689   **Anachronistic Vibration**

Mid-night full moon in September,
Bright white and brilliantly golden,
It is the season of autumn harvest,
And the Mid-Autumn Festival,
The leap year of May in Lunar calendar,
Throw me off by a month cycle.

Was the calendar maker reckless or wise?
Trying to fool a foolish man's hype.
I am a practical and simple-minded man,
Preferring Julian calendar of counting days,
From noon to noon, not mid-night to mid-night,
No week, month, year or epoch.

In the yearly autumn festivity,
Crops are nearly reaped and weather is mild,
Eating moon-cakes under the moonlight;
Tete a tete with lovers is romantic.
Old habit gets me merely wishful thinking,
I wish I were not that easily gullible.

We are all a bit nostalgic in holidays,
You lift your head to see bright moon,
Thinking of your lost youth and homeland,
We see the same moon in every corner,
It has different effect with each individual,
Not everyone is warmhearted about moonlight.

I am looking for something to cheer for,
Letting things go not worth to crying about,
Gazing across the ocean and continent,
Watching the rising and setting sun,
I am yearning for peace and contentment,
Moonlight only brings me moody and down.

Sept. 6, 2009 (MAF)

690　寓言

一位少女不穿衣裳只圍飾帶，
走在人群裡引人注目發獃，
觀眾們是如此的擾嚷狂熱，
但她卻自如的沒有紅臉。
誰敢如此公開的暴露血肉肌膚？
只有漂亮的姑娘才可鋪張門面。

裸體在鏡子前自我欣賞，
帶著一點誘人的渴望，
她胸前蓬亂的絲髮搖擺，
在她的乳房上輕輕的撫愛，
有一種未知刺激的感覺，
這是沒有人教過她的經驗。

哦！我多麼想望我是她的年齡，
隨時做她的護衛及隨員，
或者變成她身體的胸衣，
赴湯蹈火毫無埋怨，
明明知道這純粹是幻影，
終歸我不是聖賢。

我只是一位不中用的傢伙，
沒有好事可做就是做夢。
藏在我舒適的房間，
撈出所有這些同音字與謊言，
亂寫無聊的打油詩，
而世界正在倡狂混亂。

2009 年 10 月 1 日

690   **An Allegory**

A maiden wears nothing but a sash,
Walking among the crowd whips up a splash,
The gazers are in such a crush,
But she is at ease without any flush.
Who would dare to expose so much flesh?
Only pretty lass have such dash.

Naked before the mirror admiring,
With a little seductive yearning,
Her uncombed fluff hairs lightly swaying,
Caressing her breasts with a bit itching,
With an unspoken sensation of tingling,
And not taught by her teaching.

Oh! How I wish I were her age,
Ready to be her escort or page,
Or become her bodily corsage,
To fire and danger without a bit of rage,
Knowing this is only a mirage,
After all, I am not a sage.

I am only a restless old bum,
Having nothing better to do but dream,
Hiding in my comfortable room,
Whipping out all those homonyms,
Writing gibberish and ragged poem,
The world is in the pandemonium.

Oct. 1, 2009

695　不切實際的身心

如果你尚未看見我的詩，
你不會有太多損失。
我斷斷續續做過這樣多年，
就像我做很多其他的苦役，
我在人群中猛衝直撞爬來爬去，
很少人注意到我的生存。

我不是為利潤或生活而寫作，
否則我會早已餓死。
人人都說追隨你的心，
但是心缺乏意念不切實際，
很容易被不足道的親切引入陷阱，
情緒最後支付所有無益的誘惑。

心貼心，肉貼肉，
你珍惜的愈深，
你的焦慮愈重。
愛是身心的反影，
意向執行心願的鼓勵，
可憐的身體只是實行者。

我坐在陽臺聽風細訴，
他們說最好的日子已經過去，
在陰涼處真是覺得有點寒意。
我學到樹陰不完全是利他，
我自己的影子也不是真正自願，
對軟弱的頭腦又有什麼新奇？

真相往往使生活難以承受，
謊言使文明實際，
一個豔麗世界的感覺是天真。
我們不生活在一個平靜的社會，
世界上並無一切是永遠或完美，
只有死亡對命運有不明文的義務。

2009 年 10 月 4 日

695 **Impractical Heart**

If you haven't yet read my poems,
You have not missed much.
I have done this off and on for years,
Just like many of my other toils,
I dash and crawl in the jungle of man,
Few have noticed that I have ever existed.

I am not writing for profit or for survival,
I would have already starved to death,
They all say to follow your heart,
But heart is impractical and lacks of sense,
Easily trapped by those pitiful kindnesses,
Emotions end up paying for the futility.

Heart to heart, flesh to flesh,
The deeper you cherish,
The heavier is the anguishes.
Love is a reflection of mind and body,
Mind executes the urges of heart,
Poor body is only the practitioners.

I sit on my patio listening to wind murmurs,
After the last good day passes as they say,
It does feel a bit nippy in the shade.
I learned that shade from a tree is not altruistic,
Shadow from me is not truly voluntary,
What else is new to a mushy head?

Truth often makes life unbearable,
Lies make civilization realistic,
Perception of an enchanted world is naive.
We do not live in a placid society,
Nothing in this world lasts forever or perfect,
Only death is an unwritten obligation to fate.

Oct. 4, 2009

701　匆匆而過的告別

這是一個壯觀的秋天，
溫暖無風陽光四射，
秋葉不斷的下降。
我看見它們揮手告別，
在空氣中滑行輕軟低語。

我看見風景充滿顏色，
太過以飽和來欣賞它們的燦爛，
缺乏差異幾乎變得枯燥無味。
我改變了主意再看一看，
這完全變成是我年齡的特點。

我應該知道它的結果，
季節變化不是任意的步驟，
而是神秘自然的發展，
我們只能享受顯示，
不去提議我們個人的批評。

我惦念燃燒秋葉的氣味，
和冷空氣裡的股股輕煙，
舊鄉村裡的習慣久已喪失，
新法令緊緊的綁著我們的行為，
它們幾乎扼住我們的呼吸。

我們不斷進化變得非常複雜，
錯綜條款經常壓服合適的慣例，
世間永遠不會有人充分滿意，
在這世界沒有什麼是持久或完美，
僅有樹葉每年雅致的發芽與枯萎。

2009 年 10 月 13 日

701   **Transient Farewell**

It is a spectacular autumn day,
Windless, warm and clear,
Leaves continuously falling,
I almost see them waving for farewell,
Soft whispering as they glide through air.

I see the landscape full of brown color,
Too saturated to appreciate their splendor,
It is becoming monotonous without disparity.
I changed my mind giving another look,
It is becoming a trait of my old age.

I should have known the outcome,
Turning season is not a casual practice,
But a mysteriously natural process,
We can only enjoy the exhibition,
Not pass our personal judgment

I missed the smell of burning leaves,
And the wisp of smoke in chilly air,
Old country habit is long lost,
New decrees tightly bind our behavior,
They are strangling us nearly to death.

We are continuously growing into complexity,
Intricacy often overwhelms adequacy.
There will never be any personal satisfactory,
Nothing in this world lasts forever,
Only leaves sprout and wilt gracefully every year.

Oct 13, 2009

702　文明的動物園

我們都有一頭二腳，
但不享有同一性。
女性的乳房突出腹部，
男子的腹部凸出掛在鼠蹊。
添加兩者製造快樂的平坦，
扣除它們造成呆滯無吸引力。

光頭與光滑的屁股相比，
蓬鬆發光頭髮蓋著大腦皮層，
苛刻的口舌與無禮符合，
粗鹵背後的指責顫抖你的感覺。
我們忽略那些明智年長學者，
世界無知的把他們遺棄。

所有的人都有一點獸性，
不是所有的人都行動都是文明，
也不是所有的牲畜都很兇猛。
我們如何用尺度測量它們，
來確定文明與禮儀，
我的知覺僅是我的觀點。

忍耐來自經驗，
年齡不一定帶來滿足。
冷淡與自我是由於家教，
愚蠢萌芽於潛意識。
測量這些措施的特質，
是用來確定崇高與成熟度。

教學是一個學習的過程，
說謊是一個騙案的技能，
佈道是一種拌嘴的爭論。
爭吵不睦有傷身心，
只有臉依靠臉幫助睡眠，
文明的動物園仍是動物園。

2009 年 10 月 15 日

702 A Civilized Zoo

We all have two legs and one head,
But do not share the same identity.
Female breasts protrude above abdomen,
Male belly bulges out about groin.
Adding two yields an evenness of pleasure,
Subtracting them dulls the attractiveness.

Bald head competes with the smooth bottom,
Fluffy shiny hairs cover cortex of brain,
Sharp tongue coincides with rude stance,
Blunt whispers quiver your senses.
We ignore those wise aged scholars,
The world leaves them out ignorantly.

All men have a little bit of beast in them,
Not all men behave very honorably,
And not all beasts are savages.
How we measure them in the scale,
Determining civilization and civility,
My view is merely my own perception.

Endurance is acquired from experience,
Age does not always come with contentment.
Selfishness and indifference is upbringing,
Stupidity buds from our sub-consciousness.
The measurements of these traits,
Determine sainthood and maturity.

Teaching is a process of learning,
Cheating is a skill of deception,
Preaching is a form of wrangling,
Quarrelling is heart wrenching,
Only cheek to cheek helps sleep,
A civilized zoo is still a zoo keeping animals.

Oct 15, 2009

703　感覺不到的可靠性

人生就像是難以捉摸的秋霧，
為了生存和榮譽，
我們一開始就全在裡面生活，
我們知道從那裡來，
但不確實會去那裡，
我們既不能碰也聞不到它的形象，
它的意義更是含糊不清。

我坐在我的桌子前，
寫我的過去 來之不易。
早晨的陽光照過我的視窗，
給我與我的秋海棠飽食溫暖，
我手拿一杯早晨新煮的咖啡，
仍然有熱的令人愉快的氣味，
也許這就是人想像的生命。

我的心頭總是有點疑問，
誰要閱讀我平凡的生平？
我的家譜和來源又是那麼模糊，
他們就像我兒童時候鄉村的遙遠。
我父輩的生平事件是那樣可怕，
一個不受圍困的心情是快樂的心情，
艾理斯島*的登記不會有我的底細。

我赤裸的站在鏡子前面，
看的既不是我失敗或榮耀，
見到只是一個我退化的身軀，
真相的苦味並不比謊言甜，
享年給我們提供了意識，
正直或邪惡的生活都是生活，
我們都遇到相同的命運。

2009 年 10 月 28 日

　*艾理斯島，在紐約市內海，是美國早期所有歐洲移民人的入口地點。

703   **Imperceptibly Certain**

Life is as elusive as autumn mist,
We live in all of it from the beginning,
For survival and for glory,
We know where we came from,
But are not assured where we are going,
We cannot touch nor smell its form,
The meaning of it is even hazier.

I am sitting in front of my desk,
Writing my past is not coming easy.
Morning sun shines through my window,
Engulfs warmth to my begonias and me,
My morning coffee is in my hand,
Still hot with delightful scent;
Perhaps this how life is supposedly to be.

There is always doubt in my mind,
Who needs to read my colorless life story?
My family tree and root are so vague,
They are as remote as my childhood village.
The saga of my father's generation was dreadful,
A less besieged mind is a happy mind,
There is no Ellis Island registry for me.

I stand in front of a mirror naked,
Looking at neither my glory nor defeat,
Seeing only a deteriorating frame of my body,
The truth tastes bitterer than sweet lie,
Rightful age provides us awareness,
Living righteously or sinfully is living,
We all meet the same destiny.

Oct. 28, 2009

*Elise Island, just outside New York City, was an early official entry point for all European immigrants.

706　觀察

多麼溫暖與潮濕的萬聖節，
百萬個蚯蚓從它們躲藏處出現，
它們快樂的遊來滑去，
錯誤的享受它們春天的遊戲。
如果自然以欺騙性的服裝，
我能被這種溫和天氣而欺騙，
任何人都不該去責怪蚯蚓？

我們都是大自然的附屬物，
在她的符咒下糊裡糊塗的舞蹈，
我們感覺全是反應，
盲目的跟著她手指去指使。
當天氣轉變的有點涼，
我看不見其中任何一隻蚯蚓，
誰說爬蟲小頭腦不精靈？

記憶告訴我們季節的轉變，
我們不完全依靠的皮膚的感觸，
如果記憶不會提供我們需要，
昆蟲可能有正確的直覺，
除非他們有記憶的能力。
蝸牛能夠訓練去吃或不吃某些食物，
但是我們甚而不能教養我們孩子的飲食。

我相信頭腦簡單的生物，
不太信任站著步行的人類，
也許小動物有較小的影響。
我們都有一點苛刻的批評主義。
批評明顯的事和推測未知。
我們經常不是騙別人而是自己，
一個無經驗自食其果的玩客。

2009年十一月九日

706 **An Observation**

What a balmy and wet Halloween,
Millions of worms emerge from their hidings,
They are sliding and slithering joyfully,
Enjoying falsely their *spring* excursion,
If I can be fooled by such a mild day,
With Nature's deceptive costume,
How can anyone blame earthworms?

We are all collaterals in nature,
Dancing woozily under her spell,
Our sense and feeling are reflexes,
Blindly following her magic fingers.
After the weather turns a bit chillier,
I cannot see anyone of them anywhere,
Who says crawlers have small brains?

Our memory tells us the turning of season,
Not totally depending on our feeling of skin,
If memory does not serve us the need,
Insects may have the right instinct,
Unless they have the ability in remember.
Snails can be taught to eat or not to eat certain food,
But we often can't even teach our children.

I trust the simple-minded creatures,
Not too much the upright walking homo-sapiens,
Perhaps small animals have smaller influences.
We all have a bit of hypercriticism in us,
Criticize the obvious and speculate the unknown.
We often fool not others but ourselves,
An unskilled boomerang player's game.

Nov. 9, 2009

708　一個未韌化的評論

我在一堆垃圾找到一本書,
快速的掃描它的內頁或封面,
決定徹底的去閱讀。
對其內容或作者瞭解不多,
也不知道寫作的方式和語言,
這是時候我讀一點垃圾性的東西。

我去圖書館借其他的書,
它們是來自有名的評論,
一位英國寫數十本書的著名作者,
快速的讀完她贏得獎金的小說,
描述兩個維多利亞詩人的浪漫,
刺激的對話和鼓舞的詩詞。

帶著她美好對話的幻覺,
我又進一步閱讀她數本後來無味的作品,
充滿亂倫與欺騙及寄生疾病,
我非常的迷惑及不理解,
為什麼一位著名作家製作垃圾,
或許我們都感染到貪婪的病毒。

批評者就是批評者指責自負,
惡毒的譴責新作家毫無憐惜,
我也是同樣不成熟的說出觀點,
陷入一個假偽理解的陷阱,
仍然很高興找到那本在垃圾堆的書,
帶著誠意熱心的寫作。

一位朋友給我他哲學性的洞察;
「從污泥中拔出你懷疑態度的腳,
不要陷入深淵越來越深。」
孔子教了我們智慧的見解,
一個聰明的農夫不僅在高地耕作,
也知道一塊稻田裡的水有多深。

2009 年 11 月 15 日

708   **An Un-annealed Critic**

I found a book from a pile of debris,
Scanned quickly over its inner sleeve,
Decided to read thoroughly through it,
Knowing not much about its content or author,
Nor writing style and language,
It is about time I read something from rubbish.

I went to the library borrowing other books,
They came from the highly the acclaimed critics,
Of a renowned British author with dozens of books.
Devoured through her prize winning novel.
An essay of two Victorian poets' romance,
Stimulating dialogues and inspiring lyrics.

With the illusion of her good discourses,
Further read a few later tasteless writings,
Full of incest and deceit infested with disease,
I was bemused, baffled and puzzled,
Why a famous writer cranked out trash,
Perhaps we are infected by the disease of greed.

Critics are critics, judgmental and conceited,
Viciously condemning new writers without pity,
I am equally poor in giving premature opinion,
And fall into the trap of a quick pseudo-wit.
But delighted for the book from the heap of rags,
Warmhearted writing comes with sincerity.

A friend offers his philosophical insight;
Withdraw your skeptical feet from the sludge,
Not sinking deeper and deeper into the abyss.
Confucius has taught us the art of wisdom,
A wise peasant ploughs not only on high land,
But also knows the depth of a rice paddy.

Nov. 15, 2009

709　作者的悲歌

地球不失去節奏的旋轉，
生活全然與陰鬱的平靜。
我盯著我閃爍銀幕，
鍵盤沉默手指不動。
忽略政治上的爭辯和吵鬧，
能寫的事物必須是創造性。

迷人的文章和衷心詩詞，
科學的旋律和技術的發明，
教學的意圖和生活經驗，
個人災難和家庭的痛苦，
我們都背著自己的行李，
*創意寫作*座談會創建安慰。

寫作要求熱情和情緒，
自力達到期望是重要的元素，
渴望是我們助長的匪徒，
它監禁我們的思維和信仰，
我們所寫在最後會纏住我們，
取消按鈕通常不能復原。

意識就像一個被俘獲的飛蛾，
糾纏的粘在蜘蛛網上，
不斷努力的掙扎突破，
展望暗淡機會渺小，
你必須要切割絲網，
成功與失敗接合在一齊。

優異的作家通常是正直與罕見，
當他們越來越受歡迎及著名，
他們就變成出版商的木偶，
或成為搖錢吸血的僵屍，
他們改修一點內容和人物，
開始污染文學伊甸園。

2009年十一月二十九日

709   **A Writer's Lamentation**

The earth is rotating with no missing beat,
Life is utterly and lugubriously uneventful.
I am staring at my flashing screen,
Fingers are still and keyboard silent.
Ignoring political haggling and squabbling,
Things left to write have to be inventive.

Enchanted essays and hearty poems,
Scientific tunes and technical inventions,
Pedagogic intentions and life experiences,
Personal woes and family agonies,
We all bear our own baggage,
Creative Writing forum creates relief.

Writing requires passion and sentiment,
The vital ingredients for self-fulfillment,
Desire is the culprit of our abetment,
It imprisons our thinking and belief,
What we write will haunt us at the end,
Undo buttons often cannot do the undone.

Awareness is like an entrapped moth,
Entangled on the sticky spider's web,
Endlessly struggling for a breakthrough,
Prospect is dim and chance is minimal,
You will have to cut through the mesh,
Success is coalesced with failure.

Great writers are rare and usually upright,
Once becoming popular and famous,
They are puppets of those publishers,
Or turn into money-sucking zombies,
With revamped contents and characters,
They start polluting the literary Eden.

Nov. 29, 2009

711　一個假日前的情操

葉子光禿的樹幹，
風悽涼的吹著樹枝，
敵對的呼嘯通過赤裸的小枝。
它們裸露但不是死，
只是應得一點休息。

它們的根堅定的掌握，
吸收營養及豐富土壤，
昆蟲及螞蟻從它們骨肉取得營養，
葉子滋養飛蛾枝杆供給鳥築巢，
它們開花結果製造陰涼。

我們狠心殘害它們，
為了我們短暫的歡樂和榮耀，
從不會為它們的福利著想，
沒有它們慈善的威嚴，
我們就像雜草在曠野裡蔓延。

我們以砍樹慶祝聖誕，
它需要多年成長和發展，
但只是在假日短暫顯耀。
我們為什麼不在洛克菲勒中心種棵樹？
也許那樣就沒有新穎性的吹噓。

我們快樂的圍著它歌唱與跳舞，
欣賞燈光，裝飾及盛觀，
可憐的樹根暗淡的留在那兒腐爛，
貓頭鷹與鳥兒們無處藏身，
誰會聽見被砍掉樹的呻吟？

2009年十二月二日

洛克菲勒中心聖誕樹點燈慶祝儀式令我看見樹的另一面。

711   **A Pre-holiday Sentiment**

Between the stripped boughs,
Wind mournfully blows branches,
Sourly whistles through naked twigs.
They are bare not dead,
Just taking a little bit of rest.

Their roots still firmly grip,
Feeding nutrients and enriching soil,
Insects and ants nourish from their flesh,
Leaves for moths and limbs for nests,
They bear fruits and make shade.

We are heartlessly mutilating them,
For our momentary pleasure and glory,
Never thinking about their welfare,
Without their benevolent majesty,
We are stalking in the wilderness like weeds.

We celebrate Christmas by cutting trees,
It takes years for them to grow into maturity,
But only display a short while in the holidays.
Why can't we plant a tree in Rockefeller Center?
Perhaps there is nothing to brag about its novelty.

We are joyfully singing and dancing around it,
Enjoying lights, decorations and pageantry,
The poor stump left there to rot in its bleak fate,
Owls and birds lost their sanctuary,
Who would hear the moaning of a hacked tree?

Dec. 2, 2009

    Tree-lighting Ceremony in Rockefeller Center led me to see the different perspective of trees.

715　冬至的感嘆

太陽低掛在地平線上，
在它尚未溫暖和明亮之前，
它已變成黃昏的曙光。
雪覆蓋了整個的地面，
如果您希望有一個白色聖誕，
你就應該接受它的附帶，
冬季今天才真正開始，
它已經像貨車兇猛的衝擊我們。

冷就是冷、可見或是不見，
有沒有看見只是一種比喻。
它使你難以呼吸僵硬你的後頸，
像麻醉凍結你的感覺，
忽略它並不減輕苦惱，
迴避只是臨時減輕痛苦，
我們已經嘗試到它的殘忍，
僅有聖誕燈火提升我們的精神。

我欣賞看歡樂的氣氛，
觀看絕望的購物者娛樂我自己，
但不很興奮與其具來的狂風。
我要求祝福但並不謙卑，
那有免費餐飯而沒有附加的條件，
我不是太傻或就是容易受騙，
一個愚蠢詩人的典型，
我的年齡還未教導我的真確性。

季節變化每年都發生，
我們住的地方有沮喪的冬天，
但又是別人快樂的時光。
我們忘記了燦爛的夏天，
也不去想他人悲慘的情景。
太陽已在回來的途中，
離春天溫暖的天日已經不遠，
冬季不是那麼暗淡及淒涼。

2009年12月21日冬至

715   **Winter Solstice's Interjection**

The Sun is hanging low above horizon,
Before it gets warm and bright,
It turns into evening twilight.
Snow is covering the ground,
If you wish to have a white Christmas,
Then accept with the coming attachment,
Official season of winter starts today,
It's already smashing us like a freight train.

Cold is cold, visible or invisible,
Seeing it or not is only a metaphor.
It is sniffing and stiffing your nape,
Freezing your senses like anesthetic,
Ignoring it does not alleviate agony,
Evading it eases only temporary suffering,
We have already tasted its brutality,
Only Christmas lights lift our spirit.

I enjoy watching the cheerful atmosphere,
And amuse myself with the despairing shoppers,
But not thrilled with the coming blustering wave.
I am asking for blessing without being humble,
There is no free meal without string attached,
I am either too foolish or too gullible,
A typical character of a nutty poet,
My age has not yet taught me veracity.

Seasonal changes are yearly occurrences,
Gloomy days in winter where we live,
Belong to someone else's cheerful time.
We have forgotten the glorious summer,
Nor think about other bitterer circumstances.
The Sun is already on its way back,
Warmer days in spring are not far behind,
Winter is not so bleak and black.

Dec. 21, 2009 on the Winter Solstice

717　人之可敬

新聞*不是大家都值得提起*，
而是傾向於榮耀的個體，
不斷的對幾個人集中注意力。
名人就像大海裡衝浪者，
托波在榮耀的前面，
破壞了游泳者高尚的樂趣。

獲得金像獎最佳的影片，
經常包含不道德與低級，
所有的人都裝作是高手，
一種炫耀和虛張聲勢的趨勢，
它聽起來口齒伶俐靈活有趣，
但缺乏信用和責任性。

批評家就像長在牆頭上的草，
順著微風東倒西歪，
他們非常主觀偏袒和濫用，
殘忍的評判在桌子另一邊的求助者，
當桌轉動對他們沒有優勢的時候，
他們嘗試到在舞臺上的苦味。

讀完了那些高度讚揚的小說，
粗俗枯燥及不足道的內容，
由讀者們的口頭推薦，
《耿濟島文學與馬鈴薯皮餅協會》，
乃是幽默與輕鬆的作品，
馬鈴薯剝皮餅的味道也很有趣。

我們居住在太陽系一個行星，
我們更該有融洽和諧的態度。
具有較高的智慧的責任，
人與動物和昆蟲應該相互存在，
但我們經常有傲慢與糊塗見解，
勢力與職權帶領我們進入瓦解。

2009 年 12 月 29 日

717   **Worthiness of Man**

NEWS is *not everyone worthily spoken,*
It tends to glorify the peak entity,
Constantly focuses on a few personalities.
Celebrities are like ocean surfers,
Spoiling the noble pleasures of swimmers,
Riding in the front of waves for glory.

The best awarded pictures from the Academy,
Often came with poor taste and immorality,
Everyone acts like an expert,
A tendency to show off and bluffing,
It sounds slick and intriguing,
With no credence and accountability.

Critics like grasses grow on the top of walls,
Waving side to side in the breeze,
They are subjective, biased and abusive,
Judge those cruelly on the other side of table,
When the table turns not to their advantage,
The taste is bitter when they are on the stage.

After reading those highly praised novels,
But vulgar and worthless contents,
By the word of mouth from readers to readers,
The Guernsey Literary and Potato Peel Pie Society,
By far a humorous and delightful writing,
The taste of a potato peeled pie is intriguing.

There is only one planet we reside on,
We could be more cordial in attitude,
With a responsibility of higher intellectual,
Man should coexist with plants and animals.
We are often arrogant with a muddled opinion,
Power and authority lead us to downfall.

Dec 29, 2009

718　面目不明的領域

這個世界有許多表情,
有人帶著「猶大」的臉,
背叛自己的靈魂與相信,
其他隱蔽著沉重的面紗,
如今甚至在網路裡沒有臉面。
它們貌似真實的藝術,
我們成為他們欺騙的奴隸。

我們的福利是在繩線的尾端,
縫織機輕微的顫抖,
或滑梭稍有一點拖拉,
我們生命就跳躍到快速旋轉。
我們認為我們是自己的主人,
生死超出我們的計算,
地位的和年齡不在方程式裡。

我對閒聊沒有一點技巧,
直言不諱坦白的述說,
可能嚇了他們而引起迴避。
這可能也是很好的方式,
剷除雜草並保存榆樹,
或者我實在是古板守舊又乾脆,
缺失甜言蜜語的要素,

當我們在一個嚴寒的冬季,
別的地方卻有一個溫和的夏天,
我穿上柔軟睡衣上床,
聞著我絨被的和睦,
戰士們睡在壕溝裡頭帶鋼盔,
嘗試戰爭的槍彈及危險,
時空才能決心我們的命運。

2009 年 12 月 30 日

718 Faceless Domain

The world has many expressions,
Some wear the face of Judas,
Betraying their soul and believe,
Others shroud with heavy veils,
And now even faceless in the internet.
They are verisimilitude in their art,
We become slaves of their deceit.

Our welfare is at the end of a line,
A diminutive quiver by the loom,
Or a slightly tug by the shuttle,
Our life springs into fast spin.
We think we are our own master,
Live or death is beyond our calculation,
Status and age are not in the equation.

I am artless in making small talk,
Speaking frankly in a plain language,
That might scare them off avoiding me.
It may be better this way just as well,
Whacking off weeds and save the elms,
Or I am just too square or flat,
Lacking ingredients for tête-à-tête.

While we are in bitter cold winter
Somewhere else is in a balmy summer,
I put on my soft pajamas in bed,
Smelling peace in my quilt,
Soldiers sleep in bunkers with their helmets
Tasting war with guns and dangers,
Space and time determine our fate.

Dec. 30, 2009

719　罕見的時機

黑暗吞噬正規的夜晚，
風像巨人兇猛的咆哮，
把一切抓緊在它的腳下。
寒風好像不可見的箭頭，
刺穿裂縫和通過門窗，
我的房子在哀聲嘆氣，
只有我溫暖的床是超然。

我希望這不是明天的信號，
或是未來新年的是徵兆，
未來是非常神秘和匿名，
今天的禮物是往日贈品，
昨天是已往 - 就讓它過去，
我所記得的並未被忘記，
我忘掉的也不值得一提。

不是所有的願望都會實現，
新年的決議是年輕人的玩藝，
通常罕見一月內兩次滿月，
偶爾也會出現。
倒數秒針下降的時候，
月亮在雲裡隱藏她的臉，
唯一新標誌就是雪和冰雨。

我帶著舊年的擔子去睡覺，
沒有等待燈球的下降，
也未去看慶祝的煙火，
只是醒來看到垃圾淩亂的街道，
一年又安然無恙的過去，
玫瑰花車遊行每年都是相同，
我用寫作來慶祝新年。

新鮮的雪覆蓋著去年的雪，
生命在更改日曆中繼續的推進。
保證繁榮是難能可貴，
我不承擔這樣的負重是多麼美。
在新年夜罕見的第二次滿月，
帶給我既不是生命力也不是危險，

哈利路亞!慶祝快樂的新年。

719 **Once in a Blue Moon**

Dark night that devours normality,
Wind is howling as if an angry giant,
Gripping everything under its feet.
Bitter cold is like invisible arrows,
Piercing through cracks and windows,
My house is moaning and groaning,
Only my warm bed is beyond its torment.

I hope this is not a sign for tomorrow,
Or the symptom of the coming New Year,
Future is mystery and anonymity,
Today is a gift from the yesteryear,
Yesterday was past, let bygones be bygones,
What I remembered have not been forgotten,
What I forgot is not worthy of mention.

Not all wishes will come true,
New Year's resolution is beyond me,
Things do not usually happen,
Only happen once in a while in a blue moon.
At the time of counting down seconds,
The Moon is nowhere to be seen,
The only new sign is snow and sleet.

I went to bed with the old year's burden,
Did not watch for the ball descending,
Nor wait for the fireworks' celebration,
Woke up to see the littered streets,
Another year has passed peacefully.
Roses Parade in Pasadena repeats itself,
I celebrate a new beginning in my writing.

Fresh snow covers last year's snow,
Life goes on in a changed calendar.
There is no guarantee for prosperity,
How wonderful I don't carry such weight.
A rare blue moon on the New Year's Eve,
Bringing me neither peril nor vitality,

Hallelujah! A Happy New Year!

Made in the USA
San Bernardino, CA
28 April 2014